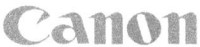

PUB. DIE-0517-000

I0481452

VIXIA GX10

4K Camcorder

Instruction Manual
NTSC

2

Trademark Acknowledgements

- SD, SDHC and SDXC Logos are trademarks of SD-3C, LLC.
- Microsoft and Windows are trademarks or registered trademarks of Microsoft Corporation in the United States and/or other countries.
- Apple, macOS are trademarks of Apple Inc., registered in the U.S. and other countries.
- HDMI, the HDMI logo and High-Definition Multimedia Interface are trademarks or registered trademarks of HDMI Licensing LLC in the United States and other countries.
- Wi-Fi is a registered trademark of the Wi-Fi Alliance.
- Wi-Fi Certified, WPA, WPA2, and the Wi-Fi Certified logo are trademarks of the Wi-Fi Alliance.
- WPS as used on the camcorder's settings, onscreen displays and in this manual signifies Wi-Fi Protected Setup.
- The Wi-Fi Protected Setup Identifier Mark is a mark of the Wi-Fi Alliance.
- JavaScript is a trademark or registered trademark of Oracle Corporation, its affiliates or subsidiaries in the United States and other countries.
- Other names and products not mentioned above may be trademarks or registered trademarks of their respective companies.
- This device incorporates exFAT technology licensed from Microsoft.
- This product is licensed under AT&T patents for the MPEG-4 standard and may be used for encoding MPEG-4 compliant video and/or decoding MPEG-4 compliant video that was encoded only (1) for a personal and non-commercial purpose or (2) by a video provider licensed under the AT&T patents to provide MPEG-4 compliant video. No license is granted or implied for any other use for MPEG-4 standard.

Highlights of the VIXIA GX10

The Canon VIXIA GX10 4K Camcorder is a high-performance camcorder whose compact size makes it ideal in a variety of situations. The following are just some of the many functions featured in the camcorder.

4K Recording

Advanced sensor and image processor
The camcorder is equipped with a 1.0-inch CMOS sensor that captures video at an effective pixel count of approximately 8.29 megapixels (3840x2160). The video is then processed by the state-of-the-art dual DIGIC DV 6 image processing platform. This allows the camcorder to excel in low-light situations and achieve improved image stabilization.

Wide zoom lens
The camcorder features a 15x optical zoom lens with a focal length at full wide angle of 25.5 mm (35 mm equivalent), offering superb wide-angle shooting capability.

Convenience and Functionality

Emphasis on versatility
This camcorder has features to make it usable as a main camera but is also small enough to be very portable. The advanced image stabilization (□ 56) will let you shoot in a variety of situations in the field.

Manual controls at your fingertips
The focus/zoom ring helps you achieve the focus you are looking for. You can easily change the ring's functionality so that you can operate the zoom. You can also assign certain frequently used functions to a customizable button and adjust those functions with the accompanying dial (□ 85). Additionally, the camcorder also features 5 assignable buttons on the camcorder and one onscreen assignable touch button to which you can assign a variety of functions to access them with ease (□ 86).

SD card recording options
The camcorder can record 4K video in MP4 format on an SD card. It is equipped with 2 SD card slots, allowing you to use dual recording (□ 43) to record the same clip on two SD cards, or relay recording to automatically switch to the other SD card when the one being used is full. Dual recording is a convenient way to create a backup of your recordings, while relay recording effectively extends the available recording time.

Network functions (□ 103)
You can connect the camcorder to a Wi-Fi network. This allows you to control the camcorder remotely from a connected network device using the Browser Remote application (□ 111) and to easily transfer files to a remote FTP server using the FTP protocol (□ 119).

Time code options (□ 68)
The time code generated by the camcorder can be output from the HDMI OUT terminal in order to synchronize it with other external devices. A user bit code (□ 70) can also be output with the output signal.

Dual Pixel CMOS AF
The camera features Dual Pixel CMOS AF technology for improved autofocus functions (□ 45). In addition to continuous AF, AF-boosted MF lets you focus manually most of the way and let the camcorder finish focusing automatically. With AF-boosted MF the camcorder does not perform unreliable focus adjustments, resulting in a smoother focusing operation than with continuous AF. The camcorder can also focus automatically on people's faces and track moving subjects while keeping them in focus (□ 50).

Even while focusing manually, the newly-added Dual Pixel Focus Guide function (□ 46) serves as a visual, intuitive guide that you can use to check if the image is in focus and the required adjustment, if it is not. This can be very helpful to ensure you always get amazingly sharp 4K video.

Creativity and Artistic Expression

Special recording modes (📖 44, 80)

When you make recordings, you can change the recording frame rate to achieve a fast or slow motion effect. Alternatively, you can use pre-recording to record 3 seconds before you decide to start recording, helping you capture those hard-to-catch opportunities.

Looks (📖 67)

You can adjust various aspects of the picture, such as the color depth, sharpness and brightness, to create a desired "look". If you prefer, you can use one of the preset looks offered. The [Wide DR] look, for example, applies a gamma curve with a very wide dynamic range and an appropriate color matrix.

Other Features

- Battery packs compatible with Intelligent System give you an estimate (in minutes) of the remaining recording time.
- Compatibility with the optional GP-E2 GPS Receiver to geotag your recordings (📖 82).
- Multiple image stabilization options (📖 56) to match your recording conditions.
- Compatibility with the optional RC-V100 Remote Controller (📖 81) when you need a professional level of remote control far surpassing that of the supplied wireless controller.
- Clear, adjustable LCD panel (📖 21) and adjustable viewfinder (📖 21) for ease of use regardless of the recording angle.

Table of Contents

6

About this Manual

Thank you for purchasing the Canon VIXIA GX10. Please read this manual carefully before you use the camcorder and retain it for future reference. Should your camcorder fail to operate correctly, refer to *Troubleshooting* (□ 129).

Conventions Used in this Manual

- ● IMPORTANT: Precautions related to the camcorder's operation.
- ⓘ NOTES: Additional topics that complement the basic operating procedures.
- □: Reference page number within this manual.
- The following terms are used in this manual:
  "Memory card" refers to an SD, SDHC or SDXC card.
  "Screen" refers to the LCD screen and the viewfinder screen.
  "Clip" refers to a single movie unit recorded with a single recording operation (for example, from the point when the REC button is pressed to start recording until it is pressed again to stop).
  "Network device" refers to a device (like a smartphone or tablet) connected to the camcorder via Wi-Fi.
- The photos included in this manual are simulated pictures taken with a still camera. Some screenshots have been altered to make them easier to read.
- Operating mode icons: A shaded icon (like CAMERA) indicates that the function described can be used in the operating mode shown; a non-shaded icon (like   ) indicates that the function cannot be used.

Position of the POWER switch: shooting (CAMERA) or playback (MEDIA) mode.
For details, refer to *Turning the Camcorder On and Off* (□ 25).

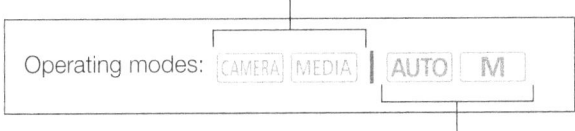

Operating modes: CAMERA MEDIA | AUTO M

Position of the mode switch. For details refer to *Changing the Camcorder's Operating Mode* (□ 26).

- The following style is used to represent menu selections. For a detailed explanation on how to use the menus, refer to *Using the Menus* (□ 32). For a summary of all available menu options and settings, refer to *Menu Options* (□ 121).

8

The menu page number is given only for main procedures.

This indicates to press the MENU button.

1 Select [Internal/External Rec].
   MENU ❯ [⬚ 1 Recording Setup] ❯ [Internal/External Rec]
2 Touch ['🎥 Internal Rec Priority] and then touch [✖].

Brackets [ ] indicate text as it appears on the camcorder's screen (menu options, onscreen buttons, messages, etc.).

This arrow indicates a deeper level in the menu hierarchy or the next step in a procedure.

Supplied Accessories

The following accessories are supplied with the camcorder:

9

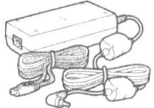

CA-946 AC Adapter
(incl. power cord)

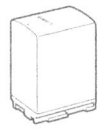

BP-828 Battery Pack

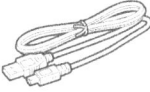

IFC-300PCU/S USB Cable

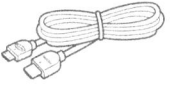

HTC-100/SS High Speed HDMI
Cable

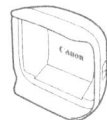

Lens hood with lens barrier

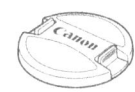

Lens cap

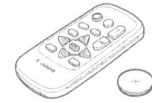

WL-D89 Wireless Controller
(incl. CR2025 lithium button
battery)

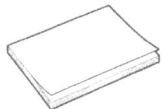

Quick Guide

Names of Parts

Camcorder

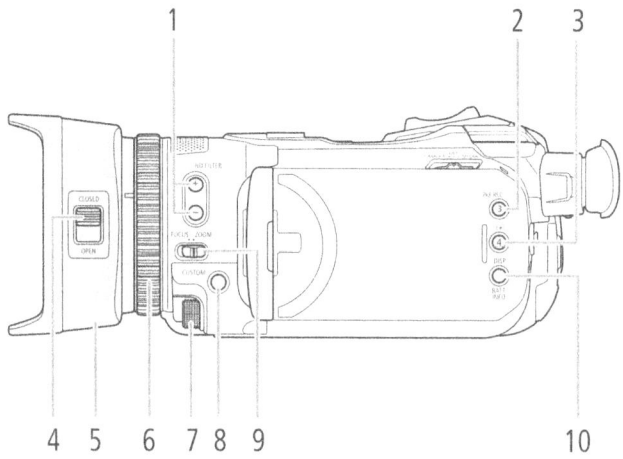

1 ND FILTER +/– buttons (□ 64)
2 PRE REC (pre-recording) button (□ 80)/
  Assignable button 3 (□ 86)
3 ⊖ (review recording) button (□ 37)/
  Assignable button 4 (□ 86)
4 Lens barrier switch (□ 35)
5 Lens hood (□ 20)
6 Focus/Zoom ring (□ 45, 52)

7 CUSTOM (customizable) dial (□ 85)
8 CUSTOM (customizable) button (□ 85)
9 Focus/Zoom ring switch (□ 45, 52)
10 DISP (onscreen display) button (□ 38)/
   BATT. INFO (battery information) button (□ 19)

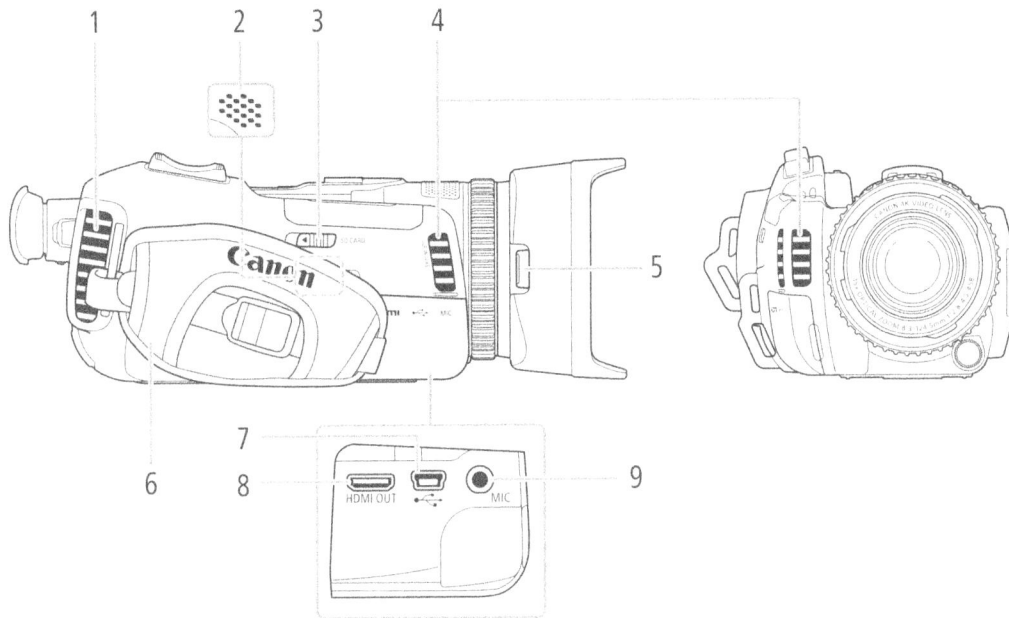

1   Exhaust ventilation outlet (□ 38)
2   Built-in speaker (□ 92)
3   SD CARD (open the SD card compartment cover) switch (□ 30)
4   Air intake vent (□ 38)

5   Lens hood release button (□ 20)
6   Grip belt (□ 22)
7   USB terminal (□ 82)
8   HDMI OUT terminal (□ 99)
9   MIC terminal (□ 72)

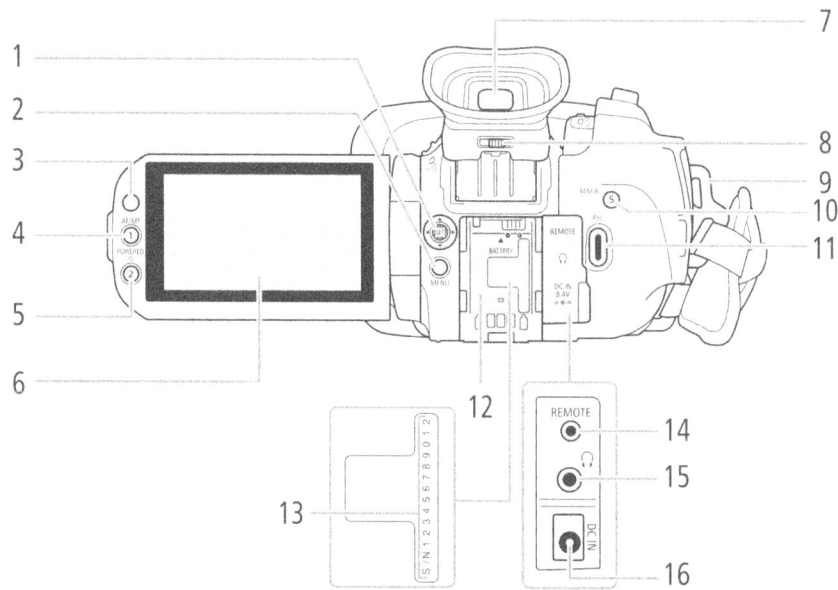

1   Joystick (📖 26)/SET button (📖 26)
2   MENU button (📖 26, 33)
3   Remote sensor (📖 24)
4   AF/MF button (📖 45)/
    Assignable button 1 (📖 86)
5   POWERED IS button (📖 56)/
    Assignable button 2 (📖 86)
6   LCD touch screen (📖 21)
7   Viewfinder (📖 21)
8   Dioptric adjustment lever (📖 21)
9   Strap mount (📖 22)

10 MAGN. (magnification) button (📖 48)/
    Assignable button 5 (📖 86)
11 REC (start/stop recording video) button (📖 35)
12 Battery attachment unit (📖 17)
13 Serial number
14 REMOTE terminal
    For connecting the optional RC-V100 Remote
    Controller (📖 81) or commercially available
    remote controllers.
15 🎧 (headphones) terminal (📖 78)
16 DC IN terminal (📖 17)

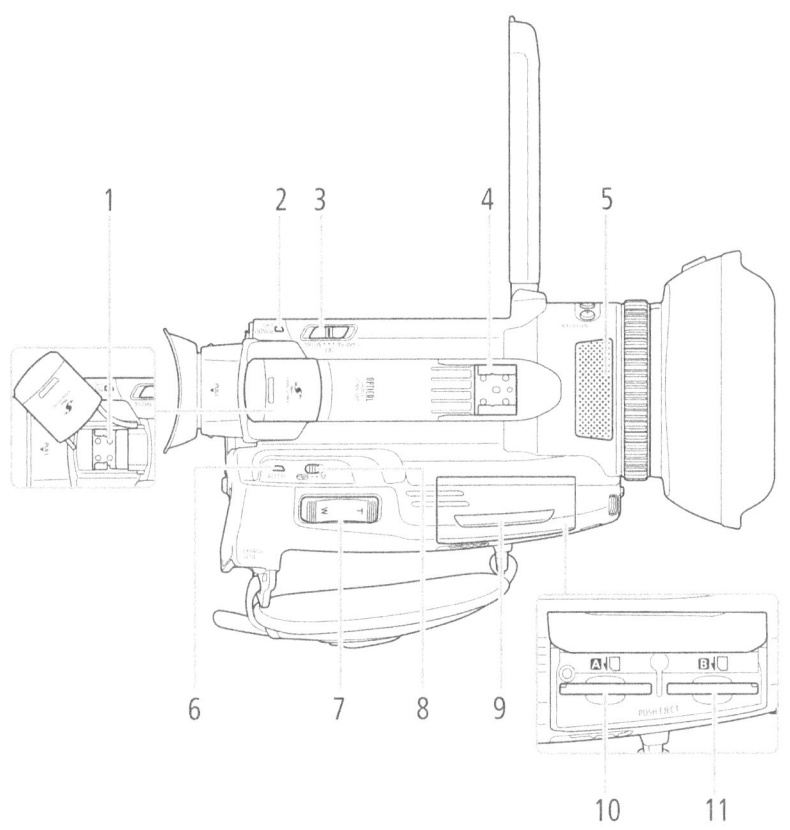

1 Mini advanced shoe (🔲 71)
2 POWER/CHG (battery charging) indicator (🔲 17)
3 Power switch (🔲 25)
4 Cold shoe
5 Built-in stereo microphone (🔲 72)

6 ACCESS indicator (🔲 35)
7 Zoom rocker (🔲 52)
8 Mode switch (🔲 26)
9 SD card compartment cover (🔲 30)
10 SD card slot **A** (🔲 30)
11 SD card slot **B** (🔲 30)

14

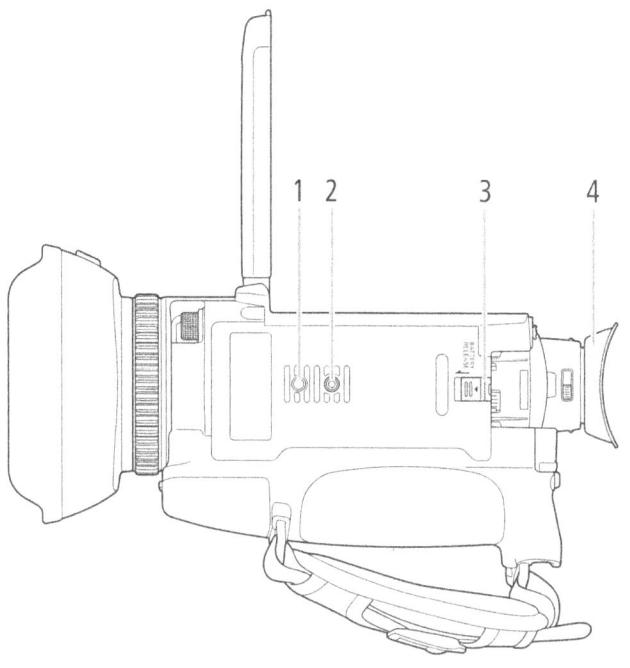

1   Socket for tripod's anti-rotation pin
2   Tripod socket (📖 24)
3   BATTERY RELEASE switch (📖 18)
4   Eye cup (📖 21)

WL-D89 Wireless Controller

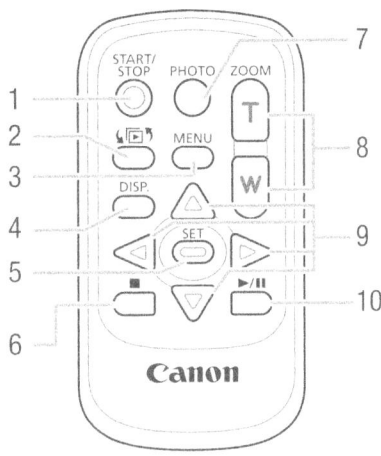

1   START/STOP button (📖 35)
    Same as the REC button on the camcorder,
    used to start/stop recording video.
2   ◣▣◥ (open the index selection screen) button
    (📖 90)
3   MENU button (📖 33)
4   DISP. (onscreen display) button (📖 38)
5   SET button

6   ◼ (stop) button (📖 90)
7   PHOTO button (📖 36)
8   Zoom buttons (📖 54)
9   Navigation buttons (▲/▼/◀/▶)
10 ▶/❙❙ (play/pause) button (📖 90)

Names of Parts

16

Preparing the Power Supply

You can power the camcorder using a battery pack or directly using the supplied AC adapter. If you connect the AC adapter to the camcorder while a battery pack is attached, the camcorder will draw power from the power outlet.

Using a Battery Pack

You can power the camcorder using the supplied BP-828 Battery Pack or the optional BP-820 Battery Pack. Both battery packs are compatible with Intelligent System so you can check the approximate remaining battery usage time (in minutes) on the screen. For more accurate readings, when using a battery pack for the first time, charge it fully and then use the camcorder until the battery pack is completely exhausted.

Charging the Battery Pack

Charge battery packs using the supplied CA-946 AC Adapter.

1 Make sure the power switch is set to OFF.
2 Connect the AC adapter's DC plug to the camcorder's DC IN terminal.
3 Connect the power cord to the AC adapter.
4 Plug the power cord into a power outlet.

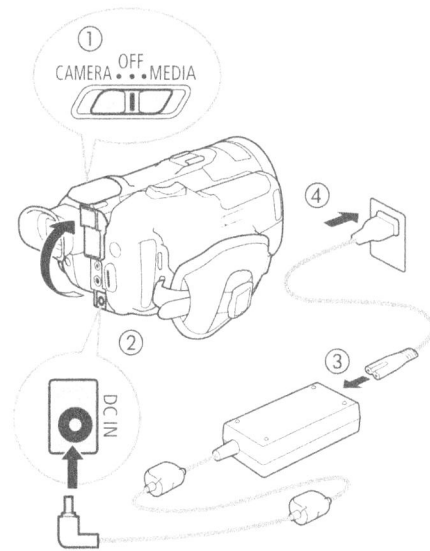

5 Attach the battery pack to the camcorder.
  • Press the battery pack softly into the battery attachment unit and slide it forward until it clicks in place.

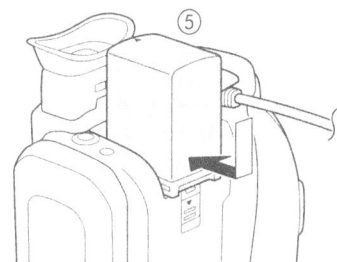

6 Charging will start.

- The POWER/CHG indicator will illuminate in red while the battery is charging. The indicator will go out when charging is completed. If the POWER/CHG indicator starts flashing, refer to *Troubleshooting* (□ 129).

POWER/CHG (battery charging) indicator

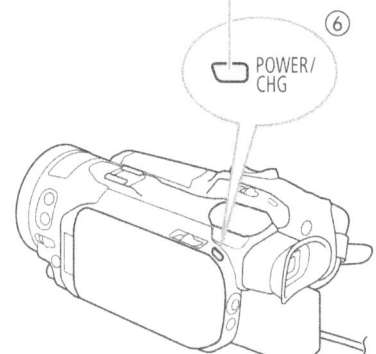

7 When charging has completed, disconnect the AC adapter in the order shown in the illustration.

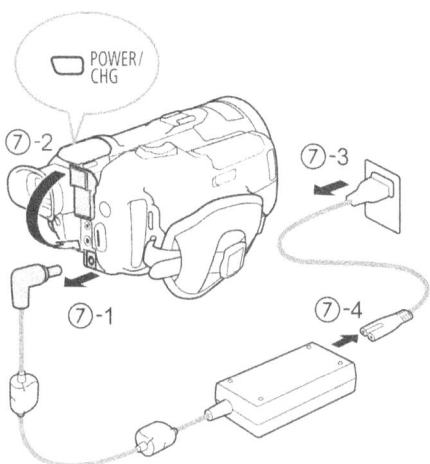

To remove the battery pack

1 Slide the BATTERY RELEASE switch in the direction of the arrow and hold it pressed down.
2 Slide the battery pack down and then pull it out.

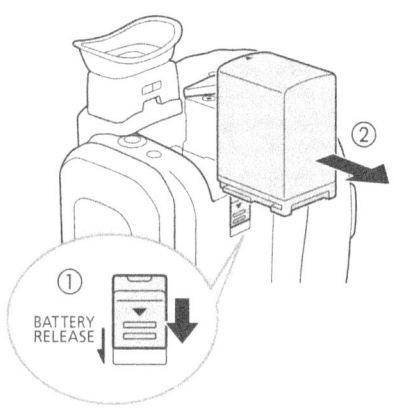

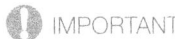 IMPORTANT

- Do not connect to the AC adapter any product that is not expressly recommended for use with this camcorder.
- Turn off the camcorder before connecting or disconnecting the AC adapter. After you turn off the camcorder, important data is updated on the SD card. Be sure to wait until the green POWER/CHG indicator goes out.
- When using the AC adapter, do not fix it permanently to one place as this may cause a malfunction.
- To prevent equipment breakdowns and excessive heating, do not connect the supplied AC adapter to voltage converters for overseas travels or special power sources such as those on aircraft and ships, DC-AC inverters, etc.

(i) NOTES

- We recommend charging the battery pack in temperatures between 10 °C and 30 °C (50 °F and 86 °F). If either the ambient temperature or the battery pack's temperature is outside the range of approx. 0 °C to 40 °C (32 °F to 104 °F), charging will not start.
- The battery pack will be charged only when the camcorder is off.
- If the power supply was disconnected while charging a battery pack, make sure the POWER/CHG indicator has gone out before restoring the power supply.
- If remaining battery time is an issue, you can power the camcorder using the AC adapter so the battery pack will not be consumed.
- For approximate charging times and recording times with a fully charged battery pack, refer to the *Reference Tables* (◻ 147, 147).
- Charged battery packs continue to discharge naturally. Therefore, charge them on the day of use, or the day before, to ensure a full charge.
- We recommend that you prepare battery packs to last 2 to 3 times longer than you think you might need.
- For handling precautions regarding the battery pack, refer to *Battery Pack* (◻ 139).

Checking the Remaining Battery Charge

With the camcorder turned off, press the BATT. INFO button to display for about 5 seconds a screen showing the approximate battery charge level and an estimate of the remaining recording time. Note that if the battery charge is too low, the battery information screen may not appear.

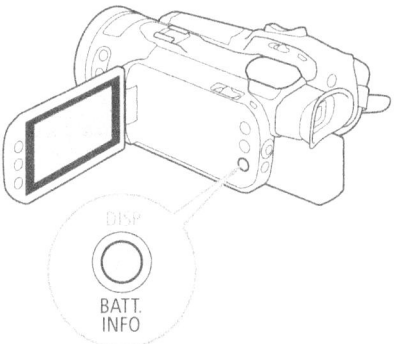

Preparing the Camcorder

This section covers the basic preparations for the camcorder such as attaching the lens hood, adjusting the viewfinder and LCD screen, and adjusting the grip belt.

IMPORTANT

- Be careful not to drop the camcorder when attaching, removing or adjusting the various accessories. Using a table or other stable surface is recommended.

Using the Lens Hood and Lens Cap

While recording, the supplied lens hood with lens barrier is effective for reducing stray light that can be the cause of lens flare and ghost images. Additionally, closing the lens barrier can help prevent fingerprints and dirt accumulation on the lens.

To carry/transport the camcorder or store it after use, remove the lens hood and place the lens cap back on the camcorder.

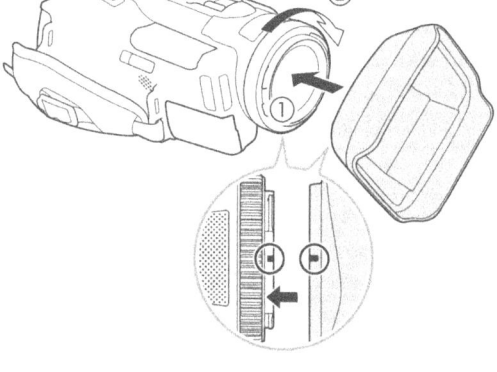

1 Remove the lens cap.

- The lens cap and lens hood cannot be used simultaneously.

2 Place the lens hood on the front of the lens so that the groove on the lens hood is aligned with the top of the lens (①), and then turn the lens hood clockwise until it stops with a click (②).

- Be careful not to deform the lens hood.
- Make sure that the lens hood is aligned with the thread.

To remove the lens hood

1 Press and hold the lens hood release button and turn the lens hood counterclockwise.

2 Place the lens cap back on the lens.

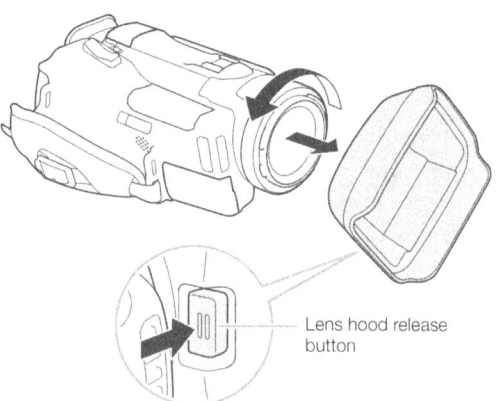

Lens hood release button

Using the Viewfinder

Adjust the position of the viewfinder to a comfortable angle. You can also adjust the diopter, if necessary.

1 Pull out the viewfinder and adjust the viewing angle.

2 Turn on the camcorder (□ 25).

3 Adjust the viewfinder using the dioptric adjustment lever.

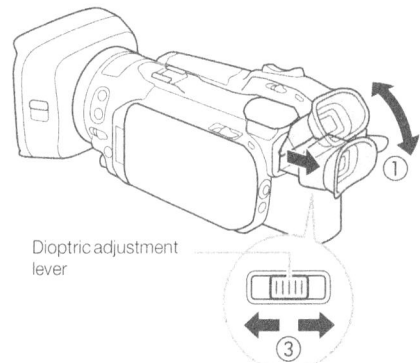

Dioptric adjustment
lever

(i) NOTES

- Make sure you keep the eye cup attached when using the camcorder.
- If you wear glasses, you may find the viewfinder easier to use if you flip back the outer edge of the eye cup toward the camcorder body.

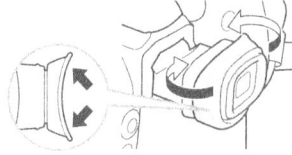

Using the LCD Screen

Open the LCD panel 90 degrees.

- You can rotate the panel 90 degrees downward and 180 degrees toward the lens.

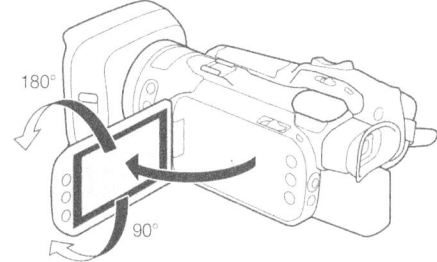

22

(i) NOTES

- You can adjust the brightness of the LCD screen with the [□ Display Setup] ❯ [LCD Brightness] and [LCD Backlight] settings in the setup menus. When the camcorder is on, you can also press and hold the DISP button for more than 2 seconds to change the [LCD Backlight] setting between [▪▪□ Normal] and [▪▪▪ Bright].
- Adjusting the brightness does not affect the brightness of recordings.
- Making the screen brighter with the [LCD Backlight] setting will shorten the effective usage time of the battery pack.
- When the LCD panel is rotated 180 degrees toward the subject, you can set [□ Display Setup] ❯ [LCD Mirror Image] in the setup menus to [**ON** On] to flip the image horizontally so it shows a mirror image of the subject.
- For details about how to take care of the LCD screen and viewfinder, refer to *Handling Precautions* (□ 138), *Cleaning* (□ 141).
- **About the LCD and viewfinder screens:** The screens are produced using extremely high-precision manufacturing techniques, with more than 99.99% of the pixels operating to specification. Less than 0.01% of the pixels may occasionally misfire or appear as black, red, blue or green dots. This has no effect on the recorded image and does not constitute a malfunction.

Adjusting the Grip Belt and Using Straps

Fasten the grip belt.

- Adjust the grip belt so that you can reach the zoom rocker with your index finger, and the REC button with your thumb.

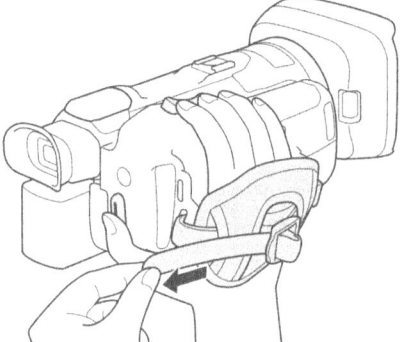

To attach an optional WS-20 Wrist Strap

To attach an optional SS-600/SS-650 Shoulder Strap

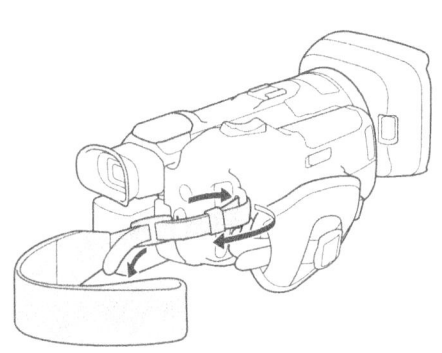

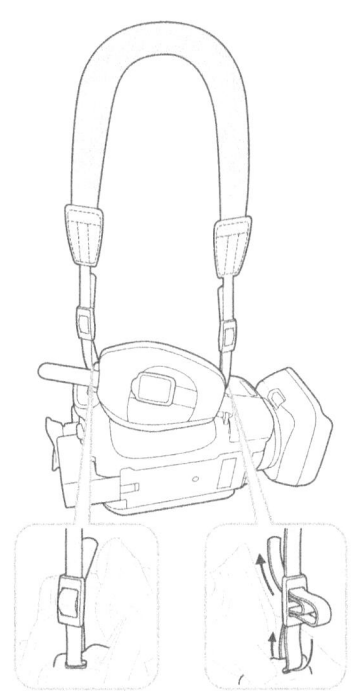

Wireless Controller

First, insert the supplied CR2025 lithium button battery into the wireless controller.

1 Press the tab in the direction of the arrow and pull out the battery holder.

2 Place the lithium button battery with the + side facing up.

3 Insert the battery holder.

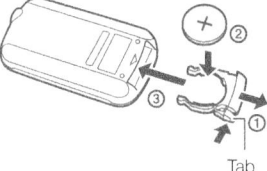

Tab

To use the wireless controller

Point the wireless controller at the camcorder's remote sensor when you press the buttons.

• You can rotate the LCD panel 180 degrees to use the wireless controller from the front of the camcorder.

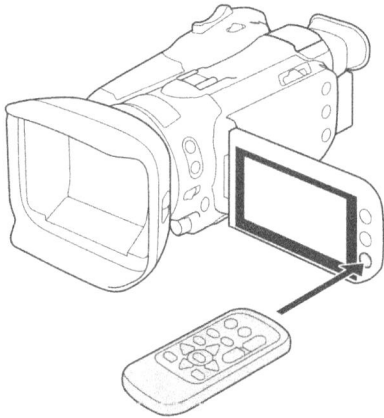

(i) NOTES

• When the camcorder cannot be operated with the wireless controller, or when it can only be operated at very close range, replace the battery.
• The wireless controller may not work properly when the remote sensor is situated under strong light sources or direct sunlight.

Using a Tripod

You can mount the camcorder on a tripod but do not use tripods with mounting screws longer than 6 mm (0.24 in.) as this may cause damage to the camcorder.

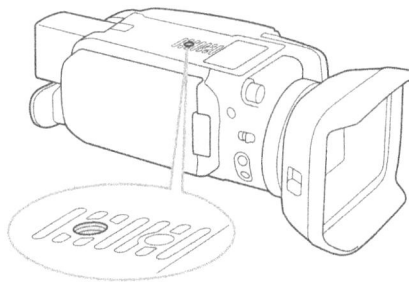

Basic Operation of the Camcorder

Turning the Camcorder On and Off

The camcorder has two basic modes: CAMERA ([CAMERA]) mode for making recordings or MEDIA ([MEDIA]) mode for playing back recordings. Select the operating mode using the power switch.

To turn on the camcorder

Set the power switch to CAMERA for [CAMERA] mode (□ 35) or MEDIA for [MEDIA] mode (□ 89).

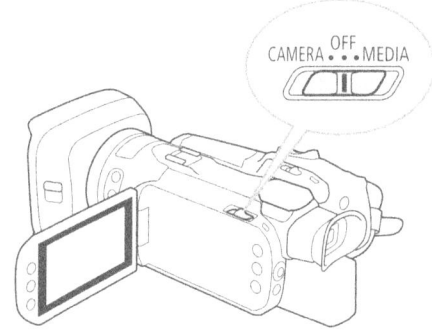

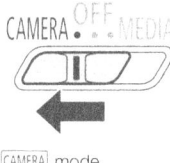

[CAMERA] mode

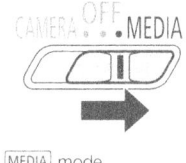

[MEDIA] mode

To turn off the camcorder

Set the power switch to OFF.

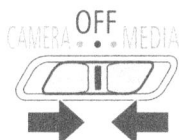

ⓘ NOTES

• When you turn on the camcorder, the POWER/CHG indicator will illuminate in green. You can set [♥ System Setup] ❯ [POWER LED] in the setup menus to [OFF Off] so the power indicator does not illuminate.

Changing the Camcorder's Operating Mode

In CAMERA mode, you can further select the camera mode to match your shooting style.

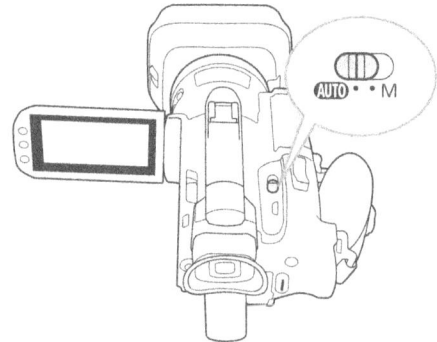

AUTO (Auto) mode

Set the mode switch to AUTO. With this mode, the camcorder takes care of all the settings while you concentrate on recording. This operating mode is suitable if you just prefer not to bother with detailed camcorder settings.

M (Manual) mode

Set the mode switch to **M**. With this mode, you can enjoy full access to menus, settings and advanced functions.

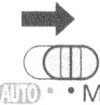

Using the MENU Button and Joystick

You can navigate some of the camcorder's menus and screens using the MENU button and joystick instead of using the touch screen.

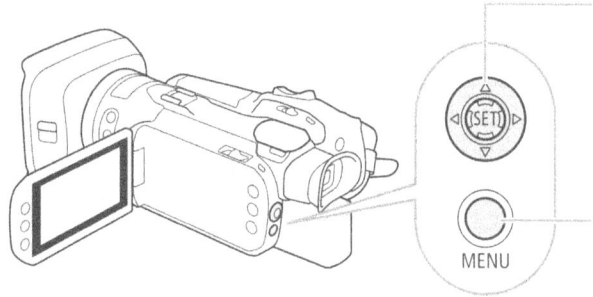

Joystick/SET button
When making a menu selection, push the joystick to move the orange selection frame in the menu. Then, press the joystick itself (in the manual, "press SET") to select the menu item indicated by the orange selection frame.

MENU button
Press the button to open the setup menus and then press again to close the menu after adjusting desired settings.

Date, Time and Language Settings

Setting the Date and Time

You will need to set the date and time of the camcorder before you can start using it. The [Date/Time] screen will appear automatically when the camcorder's clock is not set.

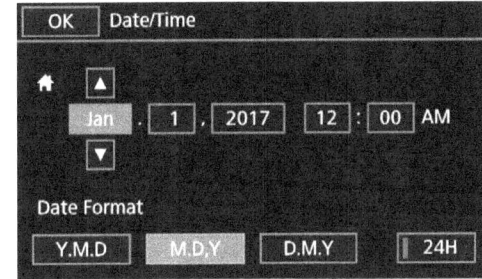

Operating modes: CAMERA MEDIA | AUTO M

1 Turn on the camcorder.
   • The [Date/Time] screen will appear.

2 Touch a field you want to change (year, month, day, hours or minutes).
   • You can also push the joystick (◄►) to move between the fields.

3 Touch [▲] or [▼] to change the field as necessary.
   • You can also push the joystick (▲▼) to change the field.

4 Set the correct date and time by changing all the fields in the same way.

5 Touch [Y.M.D], [M.D,Y] or [D.M.Y] to select the date format you prefer.
   • You can also push the joystick to select the desired button and press SET to confirm. The same is true for the rest of the steps in this procedure.
   • In some screens, the date will be displayed in short form (numbers instead of month names or only the day and month), but it will still follow the order you selected.

6 Touch [24H] to use 24-hour clock or leave it unselected to use 12-hour clock (AM/PM).

7 Touch [OK] to start the clock and close the setup screen.

ⓘ NOTES

• With the following settings, you can change the time zone, date and time also after the initial setup. You can also change the date format and clock format (12 or 24 hours).
   - [✿ System Setup] ❯ [Time Zone/DST]
   - [✿ System Setup] ❯ [Date/Time]
• When you do not use the camcorder for about 3 months, the built-in rechargeable lithium battery may be completely exhausted and the date and time setting may be lost. In such case, recharge the built-in lithium battery (📖 140) and set the time zone, date and time again.

Changing the Language

The default language of the camcorder is English. You can set it to one of 27 languages. Some settings and onscreen displays will be displayed in English, regardless of the language setting.

The following procedure is explained using only the touch screen and an abbreviated notation explained in the following section. For a detailed explanation, refer to *Using the Menus* (□ 32).

Operating modes: CAMERA MEDIA | AUTO M

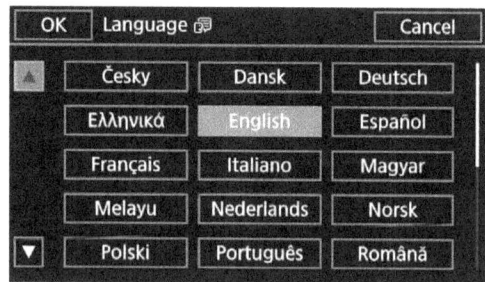

1 Select [Language 🖴].

MENU ❯ [⚘ 1 System Setup] ❯ [Language 🖴]

2 Touch the desired language and then touch [OK].

3 Touch [✕] to close the menu.

Changing the Time Zone

Change the time zone to match your location. The default setting is New York. In addition, the camcorder is able to retain the date and time of an additional location. This is convenient when you travel so that you can set the camcorder to match the time of your home location or that of your travel destination.

The following procedure is explained using only the touch screen and an abbreviated notation explained in the following section. For a detailed explanation, refer to *Using the Menus* (□ 32).

Operating modes: CAMERA MEDIA | AUTO M

1 Select [Time Zone/DST].

MENU ❯ [⚘ 1 System Setup] ❯ [Time Zone/DST]

2 Touch [🏠] to set the home time zone, or [✈] to set the time zone of your destination when you are traveling.

3 Touch [◀] or [▶] to set the desired time zone. If necessary, touch [☀] to adjust for daylight saving time.

4 Touch [✕] to close the menu.

Using SD Cards

The camcorder records clips and photos on commercially available Secure Digital (SD) cards[1]. The camcorder has two SD card slots and you can use two SD cards (in the manual, "SD card A" and "SD card B") to record on both simultaneously or to automatically switch to the other SD card when the SD card in use is full (43). Initialize SD cards (31) using the [Complete Initialization] option when you use them with this camcorder for the first time.

[1] The SD card is used also to save menu settings files.

Compatible SD Cards

The following types of SD cards[2] can be used with this camcorder. For the latest information about SD cards tested for use with this camcorder, visit your local Canon Web site.

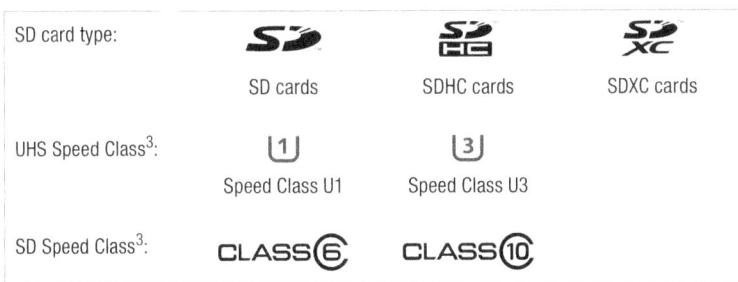

[2] As of June 2017, the clip recording function has been tested using SD cards made by Panasonic, Toshiba and SanDisk.
[3] UHS and SD Speed Class are standards that indicate the minimum guaranteed data transfer rate of SD cards.
To record 4K clips with a resolution/bit rate of [3840x2160 (150 Mbps)] (42) or using slow & fast motion recording (44), we recommend using SD cards rated UHS Speed Class U3.

IMPORTANT

- About SDXC cards: You can use SDXC cards with this camcorder but SDXC cards are initialized by the camcorder using the exFAT file system.
    - When using exFAT-formatted cards with other devices (digital recorders, card readers, etc.), make sure that the external device is compatible with exFAT. For more information on compatibility, contact the computer, operating system or card manufacturer.
    - If you use exFAT-formatted cards with a computer OS that is not exFAT-compatible, you may be prompted to format the card. In such case, cancel the operation to prevent data loss.
- After repeatedly recording, deleting and editing clips (if the SD card is fragmented), you may notice slower writing speeds to the card and recording may even stop. In such case, save your recordings and initialize the card with the camcorder using the [Complete Initialization] option. Be sure to initialize SD cards especially before shooting important scenes.

NOTES

- Proper operation cannot be guaranteed for all SD cards.

29

Inserting and Removing an SD Card

1 Turn off the camcorder.
   • Make sure the POWER/CHG indicator is off.

2 Open the SD card compartment cover.
   • Slide the SD CARD switch all the way in the direction of the arrow to open the cover.

3 Insert the SD card straight, with the label facing away from the right side of the camcorder (the side with the air intake vent), all the way into one of the SD card slots until it clicks.
   • You can also use two cards, one in each SD card slot.
   • To remove an SD card, make sure the ACCESS indicator is off and then push the card once to release it. When the SD card springs out, pull it all the way out.

4 Close the SD card compartment cover.
   • Do not force the cover closed if the SD card is not correctly inserted.

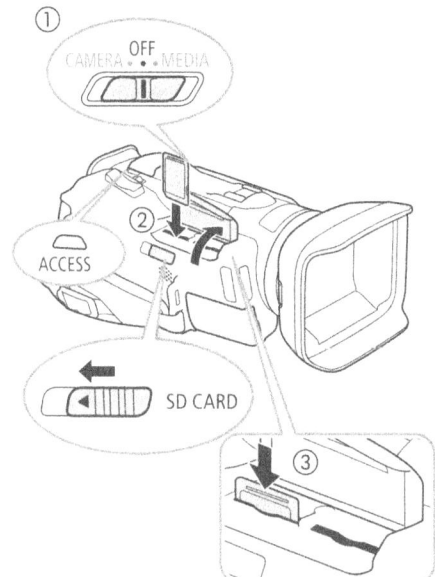

ACCESS (SD card access) indicator

SD card access indicator	SD card status
Red (on or flashing)	Accessing the SD card(s).
Off	Neither SD card is being accessed or no SD cards are inserted in the camcorder.

🛈 IMPORTANT

• Observe the following precautions while the ACCESS indicator is illuminated in red. Failure to do so may result in permanent data loss.
  - Do not disconnect the power source or turn off the camcorder.
  - Do not open the SD card compartment cover.
  - Do not change the camcorder's operating mode.
• Turn off the camcorder before inserting or removing an SD card. Inserting or removing a card with the camcorder on may result in permanent data loss.
• SD cards have front and back sides that are not interchangeable. Inserting an SD card facing the wrong direction can cause a malfunction of the camcorder. Be sure to insert the SD card as described in step 3.
• SD cards have a physical switch to prevent writing on the card so as to avoid the accidental erasure of the card's content. To write-protect the SD card, set the switch to the LOCK position.
• If you set [System Setup] ❯ [ACCESS LED] to [OFF Off], the ACCESS indicator will not illuminate.

Initializing an SD Card

Initialize SD cards when you use them with this camcorder for the first time. You can also initialize a card to permanently delete all the recordings it contains.

The following procedure is explained using only the touch screen and an abbreviated notation explained in the following section. For a detailed explanation, refer to *Using the Menus* (□ 32).

Operating modes: CAMERA MEDIA | AUTO M

1 Power the camcorder using the AC adapter.
- Do not disconnect the power source or turn off the camcorder until the initialization is completed.

2 Select [Initialize] for the desired SD card.
MENU ❯ [⚙ 2 * Recording Setup] ❯ [Initialize SD] ❯ [A Mem. Card A] or [B Mem. Card B] ❯ [Initialize]
* Page 1 in MEDIA mode.
- In the initialization screen, touch [Complete Initialization] to physically erase all the data rather than just clear the file allocation table of the SD card.

3 Touch [Yes].
- If you selected the [Complete Initialization] option, you can touch [Cancel] to cancel the initialization while it is in progress. You can use the SD card but all data will be erased.

4 When the confirmation message appears, touch [OK] and then touch [✖].

IMPORTANT

- Initializing an SD card will permanently erase all recordings. Lost data cannot be recovered. Make sure you save important recordings in advance (□ 101).
- Depending on the SD card, the complete initialization may take up to a few minutes.

Selecting the SD Card for Recordings

You can select the SD card on which clips and photos will be recorded.

The following procedure is explained using only the touch screen and an abbreviated notation explained in the following section. For a detailed explanation, refer to *Using the Menus* (□ 32).

Operating modes: CAMERA | AUTO M

1 Select [Recording Media].
MENU ❯ [⚙ 1 Recording Setup] ❯ [Recording Media]

2 Touch the desired SD card ([A Mem. Card A] or [B Mem. Card B]) for recording clips ([🎥 Rec Media for Movies]) and/or photos ([📷 Rec Media for Photos]).

3 Touch [✖].
- After closing the menu, the icon of the SD card selected for recording clips will appear on the screen.

Using the Menus

The camcorder's functions can be adjusted from the setup menus, accessed by pressing the MENU button, or from the FUNC menu, accessed by touching or selecting the onscreen [FUNC] button. For details about the available menu options and settings, refer to *Menu Options* (📖 121).

Throughout the rest of this manual, functions are explained using touch operations but menu settings can be equally accessed using the joystick and SET button. The following procedures explain how to use both methods. If necessary, refer back to this section for details on using the joystick.

FUNC Menu

In ⟨CAMERA⟩ mode, the FUNC menu offers a quick way to control various shooting related functions such as white balance, exposure, focus, etc. Available functions are more limited in ⟨AUTO⟩ mode.

To use the touch panel

FUNC menu in ⟨ M ⟩ mode

1 Touch [FUNC] on the shooting screen.

2 Touch the icon of the desired function on the left column.
   • If necessary, touch [∧]/[∨] to scroll up/down.

3 Touch the icon of the desired setting on the bottom row.

4 Touch [✕] to close the FUNC menu or [↩] to return to the left column.

To use the joystick

1 On the shooting screen, push the joystick to select [FUNC] and then press SET.

2 Push the joystick (▲▼) to select the desired icon from the left column and then press SET.

3 Push the joystick (◀▶) to select the desired icon from the bottom row and then press SET.
   • To select a value from an adjustment dial, first push the joystick (▼) to highlight the dial in orange and then (◀▶) to select the desired value.

4 Select [✕] to close the FUNC menu or [↩] to return to the left column.
   • From the left column, push the joystick (▶) to select the [✕] icon and then press SET. From the bottom row, push the joystick (▲) once and then (◀▶) to select the desired icon.

ⓘ NOTES

• Depending on the selected function, other buttons, adjustment dials, and other controls may appear on the screen. These are explained in the respective section of the manual.

Setup Menus

Following is a step-by-step explanation of how to select a typical option from the setup menus. Some menu items may require additional steps. Such operations will be explained in the respective section of the manual. For brevity's sake, references to menu settings throughout the manual may be abbreviated as follows:

MENU ❯ [**Y** 1 System Setup] ❯ [Language 🖅] ❯ Desired option

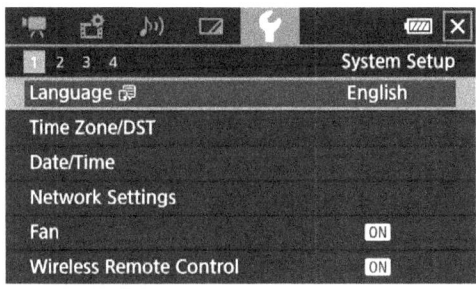
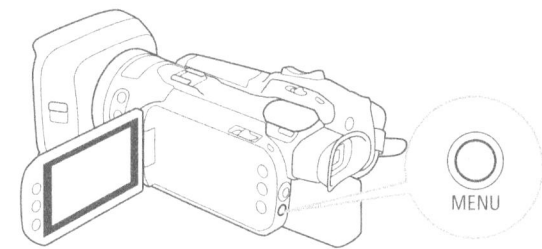

To use the touch panel

1 Press the MENU button.

2 Touch the icon of the desired setup menu from the top row.

• In the example, the **Y** icon, corresponding to the [System Setup] menu.

3 Touch the desired menu item ([Language 🖅], in the example).

• If the desired menu item does not appear in the menu page displayed, drag your finger left/right to scroll through other menu pages.

• For main procedures, the page number may be given in the manual (1, in the example). If you know the page number, you can touch the number icon on the top left of the screen to open directly the desired menu page.

4 Touch the desired setting option and then touch [✕] to close the menu.

• You can touch [↩] to return to the previous menu page.

To use the joystick

1 Press the MENU button.

2 Push the joystick (◀▶) to select the icon of the desired setup menu.

• In the example, the **Y** icon, corresponding to the [System Setup] menu.

• If one of the icons in the top row is not selected when you open the menu, first push the joystick (▲▼) to move the orange selection frame to one of the icons.

3 Push the joystick (▲▼) to select the desired menu item ([Language 🖅], in the example) and then press SET.

• If the desired menu item does not appear in the menu page displayed, push the joystick (◀▶) to scroll through other menu pages.

• For main procedures, the page number may be given in the manual (1, in the example), making it easier to find the desired menu page.

4 Push the joystick (▲▼) to select the desired setting option and then press SET.

5 Press the MENU button to close the menu.

• You can push the joystick to highlight the [↩] button and press SET to return to the previous menu page. You can also highlight the [✕] button and press SET to close the menu.

(i) NOTES

• You can use the MENU button on the supplied wireless controller to open the setup menus.
• Touching [✖] or pressing the MENU button at any time closes the menu.
• Unavailable items may appear grayed out.

Recording Video and Photos

This section explains the basics of recording clips* and photos. For details on recording audio, refer to *Recording Audio* (☐ 72).

Before making important recordings for the first time, make test recordings using the video configuration(s) you plan to use to check that the camcorder operates correctly. Should the camcorder fail to operate correctly, refer to *Troubleshooting* (☐ 129).

* "Clip" refers to a single movie unit recorded with a single recording operation.

Operating modes: [CAMERA] | [AUTO] [M]

Preparing to Record

1 Attach a charged battery pack to the camcorder (☐ 17).

2 Insert a card into an SD card slot.
 • To use relay recording or dual recording (☐ 43), insert SD cards into both slots.

3 Open the lens barrier.
 • Set the lens barrier switch to OPEN.

4 If you need to use the viewfinder, pull it out and adjust it, as necessary.
 • You can use the dioptric adjustment lever and tilt the viewfinder 45 degrees upward.

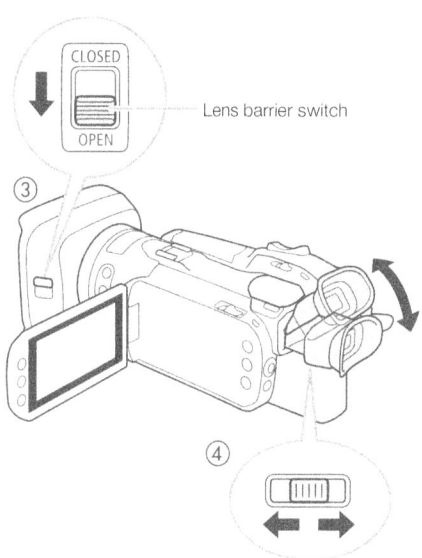

Lens barrier switch

Basic Recording

When you use $\boxed{\text{AUTO}}$ mode to shoot video and take photos, the camcorder will automatically adjust various settings for you. In $\boxed{\text{M}}$ mode, you can manually adjust the focus, exposure and many other settings according to your needs and preferences.
You can also start/stop recording video remotely using Browser Remote on a connected network device (□ 111, 115).

1 Set the mode switch to the desired position.

- Set it to **AUTO** ($\boxed{\text{AUTO}}$ mode) or **M** ($\boxed{\text{M}}$ mode), according to how you want to use the camcorder.

2 Set the power switch to CAMERA.

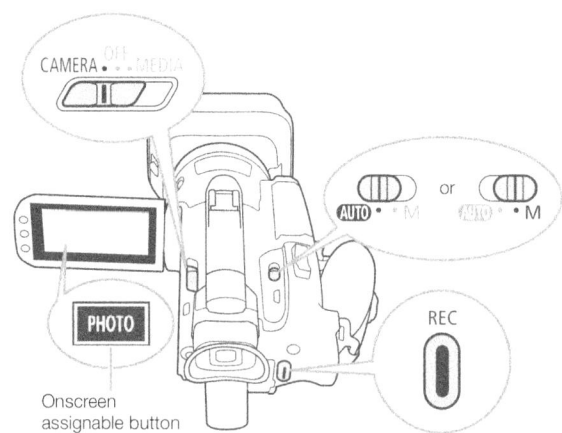

Onscreen assignable button

To record video

Press the REC button to begin recording.

- During recording, ● will appear on the screen.
- Press the REC button again to stop recording. ● will change to ■ and the clip will be recorded on the card selected for recording clips.
- You can also press the START/STOP button on the supplied wireless controller.

To take photos

Touch the onscreen assignable button (□ 86).

- By default, the [**PHOTO** Photo] function is assigned to the onscreen assignable button.
- A green ● icon will appear at the bottom of the screen. Also, at the upper right of the screen, ◘ ▶ will appear with the icon of the card selected for recording photos.
- You can also press the PHOTO button on the supplied wireless controller.

When you have finished recording

1 Set the lens barrier switch to CLOSED to close the lens barrier.

2 Make sure that the ACCESS indicator is off.

3 Set the power switch to OFF.

4 Close the LCD panel and return the viewfinder to its retracted position.

ⓘ IMPORTANT

- Observe the following precautions while the ACCESS indicator is illuminated in red. Failing to do so may result in permanent data loss or damage to the card.
  - Do not open the SD card compartment cover.
  - Do not disconnect the power source or turn off the camcorder.
  - Do not change the camcorder's operating mode.
- Be sure to save your recordings regularly (□ 101), especially after making important recordings. Canon shall not be liable for any loss or corruption of data.

(i) NOTES

- If the camcorder switches to the other SD card while recording video due to the relay recording function (□ 43), the two parts (before/after the switch) will be recorded as separate clips. With thesoftware Data Import Utility, you can join clips recorded on different SD cards and save them on a computer as a single clip (□ 101).

- When recording clips on an SDHC card, the video (stream) file in the clip will be split approximately every 4 GB. Playback with the camcorder will be continuous.

- The maximum continuous recording time of a single clip is 6 hours. After that, a new clip will be created automatically and recording will continue as a separate clip.

- When recording in bright places, it may be difficult to use the LCD screen. In such case, use the viewfinder or adjust the brightness of the screen (□ 22).

- **About the power saving mode:** When [**Ƴ** System Setup] ❯ [Auto Power Off] is set to [**ON** On], the camcorder will shut off automatically to save power when it is powered by a battery pack and is left without any operation for 5 minutes. Use the power switch to turn on the camcorder.

- When you need to record for a long time with the camcorder set on a tripod, you can close the LCD panel and use only the viewfinder in order to save power when using a battery pack (□ 21).

Reviewing the Latest Clip Recorded

You can review the last 4 seconds of the last clip recorded with the camcorder without switching to [MEDIA] mode. While reviewing the clip, there will be no sound from the built-in speaker.

1 Record video.

2 After you finish recording a clip, press the ⊜ button.

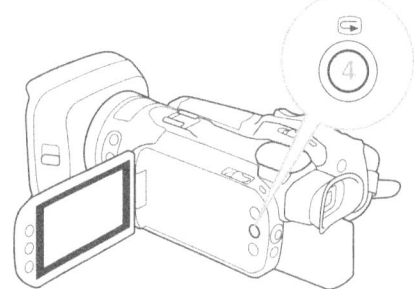

Using the Fan

The camcorder uses an internal cooling fan to reduce the camcorder's internal heat.

1 Select [Fan].

    MENU ❯ [ᕮ ① System Setup] ❯ [Fan]

2 Touch the desired option and then touch [✕].

Options

[**A** Automatic]: The fan runs while the camcorder is not recording and it is automatically turned off while the camcorder is recording video (while the ● icon appears at the top of the screen). However, if the internal temperature of the camcorder is too high, the fan will be activated automatically (in that case, **FAN** will appear next to the 🌡 icon). When the camcorder's temperature has decreased sufficiently, the fan will be turned off. Use this setting when you do not want the camcorder to pick up the fan's operating sound.

[**ON** On]:   The fan runs at all times. Use this default setting in most cases.

> ❗ IMPORTANT
>
> • While the fan is running, the exhaust vent will emit warm air.
> • Be careful not to obstruct in any way the fan's air vents (📖 11).

Onscreen Displays

Refer to this section for an explanation of the various screen displays that appear in CAMERA mode. The onscreen displays that actually appear at any time will vary depending on the current menu settings and operating mode.

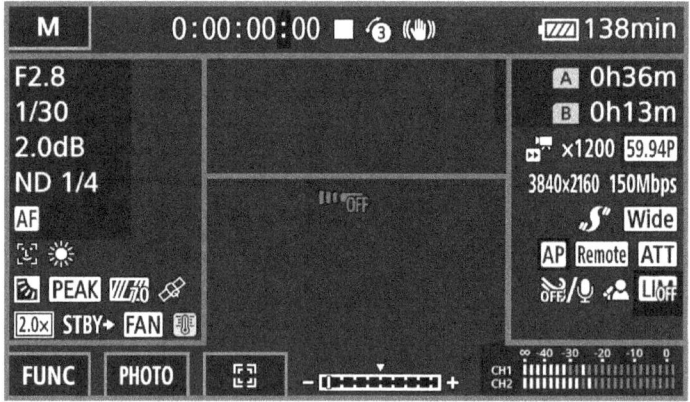

AF frames

Depending on the focus function used and AF frame size setting (□ 49), you may see some of the following AF frames.

Continuous AF frame – always in white (□ 49)
AF-Boosted MF frame – in yellow: manual adjustment range; in white: automatic adjustment range (□ 48)

Tracking: Subject selection

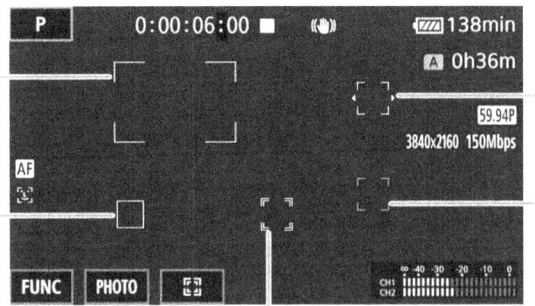

Face detection: Main subject (□ 50)

Face detection: Other face detection frames

Tracking: During tracking (□ 50)

Top of the screen

Icon/Display	Description
AUTO	AUTO mode (□ 26)
P, Tv, Av, M, 🌙, 🔦, 📷, 🔥, 🏔, 🌅, ✹, A, ☀	Shooting mode (□ 58)
00:00:00.00, 00:00:00:00	Time code (□ 68)
■, ● (in red)	Recording operation (□ 35) ■ – record standby, ● – recording
📷	Pre-recording (□ 80)
((🖐)), ((🖐)), ((🖐)) (in yellow)	Image stabilization (□ 56)
📶, 📶, 📶, 📶 (in white), 📶 (in yellow), 📶 (in red) 000 min	Remaining battery charge (□ 17) The icon shows an estimate of the remaining charge. The remaining recording time is displayed, in minutes, next to the icon. • When 📶 is displayed, replace the battery pack with a fully charged one. • Depending on the conditions of use, the actual battery charge may not be indicated accurately.
📷►A, 📷►B A⊘ (in red), B⊘ (in red)	Photo recorded (□ 36) • When A⊘ (or B⊘) is displayed, the photo cannot be recorded because of a problem with the SD card.

Left side of the screen

Icon/Display	Description
F00	Aperture value (□ 59, 59)
1/00000	Shutter speed (□ 58, 59)
AE ±0 0/0 (in orange)	Exposure compensation (□ 62)
±0 0/0 ✳ (in orange)	Exposure lock (□ 61)
00.0dB	Gain value (□ 59)
GAIN 00.0dB (value in orange)	AGC limit (□ 57)
ND 1/00	ND filter (□ 64)
MF, AF 000ft	Focus (□ 45) • While adjusting the focus, the estimated focusing distance will be displayed next to the icon.
🙂, 🙂	Face detection & tracking (□ 50)
☀, 🌤, K, 🔆, 🔆2	White balance (□ 65)
🔆2, 🔆3	Look (□ 67)

Icon/Display	Description
⬛	Backlight correction (🔲 62)
PEAK, **PEAK**	Peaking (🔲 47)
Z70, **Z100**	Zebra pattern (🔲 63)
✎	GPS signal (🔲 82): continuously on – satellite signal acquired; flashing – satellite signal not acquired. • Only when the optional GP-E2 GPS Receiver is connected to the camcorder.
2.0×	Digital tele-converter (🔲 55)
REC➡, STBY➡	Recording command (🔲 99)
FAN, 🌡	Fan operation and temperature warning (🔲 38) • When the camcorder's internal temperature rises above a certain level, 🌡 will appear in yellow. If the temperature rises further, 🌡 will appear in red. • When **FAN** appears in red, this indicates a fan-related warning (🔲 134).

Right side of the screen

Icon/Display	Description
Ⓐ 000h00m, Ⓑ 000h00m, Ⓐ End, Ⓑ End (icon in red)	SD card status and remaining recording time (🔲 29) In green – can record; in yellow – SD card almost full; in white – reading the SD card. • When the SD card is full, Ⓐ End (or Ⓑ End) will appear, with the icon in red, and recording will stop.
Ⓐ⊘ (in red), Ⓑ⊘ (in red)	No SD card or cannot record on the SD card.
Ⓐ↷, Ⓑ↷	Relay recording (🔲 43)
EXT **HDMI**	External recording mode (🔲 99)
YCC422, **YCC420** 00bit	Color sampling of the external recording (🔲 99)
W━I━T	Zoom bar (🔲 52) • Appears only while zooming.
0000x0000	Resolution (🔲 42, 99)
59.94P, **29.97P**, **23.98P**	Frame rate (🔲 42, 99)
000Mbps	Bit rate
▸x0.00, ▸x0000	Slow & fast motion recording (🔲 44)
S	Optional accessory connected to the mini advanced shoe (🔲 71)
Tele, **Wide**	Settings optimized for an optional conversion lens (🔲 123)
AP **Remote**	Network type, function and connection status (🔲 103) In white - function ready to be used; in yellow - connecting to or disconnecting from a network; in red - error has occurred.
ATT	Microphone attenuator (🔲 74)
⋙/🎤, ⋙/🎤	Wind screen (🔲 75)
🎼, 🎬, 👥, 🎭, 🐦, 🔊, ♪c	Audio scene (🔲 72)
L/OFF	Audio limiter (🔲 76)
MAGN.	Magnification (🔲 48)

Bottom and center of the screen

Icon/Display	Description
[FUNC]	Opens the FUNC menu (□ 32, 121)
[⬛], [⬛], [⬛], [WB], [✸], [CH/CH], [AF/MF], [⬛], [⬛], [REC REVIEW], [MAGN], [PHOTO]	Onscreen assignable button (□ 86) • By default, the [PHOTO Photo] function (take a photo) is assigned to the button.
[⬛], [⬛OFF]	Tracking (□ 50)
–⬛⬛⬛⬛⬛⬛+	Exposure bar (□ 59)
⬛⬛⬛⬛	Audio level meter (□ 74)
⬛OFF (in red)	Wireless controller disabled (□ 127)

41

ⓘ NOTES

• You can press the DISP button to turn off most icons and displays in the following sequence:
All displays on → Only onscreen markers (when activated, □ 126) → Minimal displays (recording operation, etc.)

Video Configuration: Resolution, Bit Rate and Frame Rate

With the following procedures you can set the video configuration used for recording clips on an SD card in the camcorder. Select the combination of resolution/bit rate and frame rate settings that best matches your creative needs. Available options for some settings may change depending on previous selections for other settings. See the table following the procedures for a summary.

Operating modes: CAMERA | AUTO M

Selecting Internal Recording

By default, the camcorder is configured to allow internal recordings on an SD card. If the camcorder was set to external recording-only mode, follow the procedure below to enable internal recording. For details about setting the video configuration for recordings using an external recorder connected to the camcorder's HDMI OUT terminal, refer to *Connecting to an External Monitor or Recorder* (🔲 99).

1 Select [Internal/External Rec].

MENU ❯ [🗗 1 Recording Setup] ❯ [Internal/External Rec]

2 Touch ['🎥 Internal Rec Priority] and then touch [✖].

Selecting the Resolution and Bit Rate

1 Select [Resolution].

MENU ❯ [🗗 1 Recording Setup] ❯ [Resolution]

2 Touch the desired option and then touch [✖].

• The selected resolution and bit rate will appear at the right of the screen.

Selecting the Frame Rate

1 Select [Frame Rate].

MENU ❯ [🗗 1 Recording Setup] ❯ [Frame Rate]

2 Touch the desired option and then touch [✖].

• The icon of the selected frame rate will appear at the right of the screen.

Available video configuration settings

Resolution (Bit rate*)	Frame rate		
	59.94P	29.97P	23.98P
3840x2160 (150 Mbps)	●	●	●
1920x1080 (35 Mbps)	●	●	●
1920x1080 (17 Mbps)	●	●	●
1280x720 (8 Mbps)**	●	—	—
1280x720 (4 Mbps)**	—	●	—

* The camcorder uses a variable bit rate (VBR).
**The frame rate is fixed and cannot be changed.

Dual Recording and Relay Recording

The camcorder features two convenient recording methods that can be used when both card slots contain an SD card: dual recording and relay recording.

Dual recording: This function records the same clip simultaneously to both SD cards, which is a convenient way to make a backup copy of your recordings while you record.

Relay recording: This function allows you to continue recording on the other SD card without interruption when the SD card you are using becomes full.

Operating modes: [CAMERA] | [AUTO] [M]

1 Select [Dual/Relay Recording].

MENU ❯ [⚙ 1 Recording Setup] ❯ [Dual/Relay Recording]

2 Touch [D Dual Recording] or [A⇨ Relay Recording] (or [B⇨ Relay Recording]) and then touch [✖].

- When dual recording is activated, the status of both SD cards will appear at the top right of the screen. When relay recording is activated, the SD card icon will change to [A⇨] (or [B⇨]).
- Touch [Standard Recording] to not use either function.

(i) NOTES

- If an SD card becomes full during dual recording, recording on both cards will stop. On the other hand, if an error occurs with one of the SD cards, recording will continue on the other card.
- With the software Data Import Utility, you can join relay clips recorded on different SD cards and save them on a computer as a single clip (□ 101).
- Relay recording is available from SD card slot A to SD card slot B, and vice versa, but the switch will be performed only once.

Slow & Fast Motion Recording

You can record clips that have a slow motion or fast motion effect during playback, simply by selecting the desired slow/fast motion rate (from x0.2 to x1200 the normal speed). Available slow/fast motion rates will vary depending on the resolution and frame rate currently selected. Sound is not recorded when slow & fast motion recording is activated.

Operating modes: CAMERA | AUTO   M

1 Select [Slow & Fast Motion].

   MENU ❯ [⊡ 1 Recording Setup] ❯ [Slow & Fast Motion]

2 Touch the desired slow & fast motion rate and then touch [✕].

   • Touch [OFF] to turn off slow & fast motion recording.

   • ☐ or ☐ and the selected rate will appear on the screen.

Available slow/fast motion rates

Resolution	Frame rate	Available slow/fast motion rates
3840x2160 (150 Mbps)	59.94P	x2, x4, x10, x20, x60, x120, x600, x1200
	29.97P	x0.5*
	23.98P	x0.8
1920x1080 (35 Mbps), 1920x1080 (17 Mbps)	59.94P	x0.5, x2, x4, x10, x20, x60, x120, x600, x1200
	29.97P	x0.25, x0.5
	23.98P	x0.2, x0.4, x0.8
1280x720 (8 Mbps)	59.94P	x2, x4, x10, x20, x60, x120, x600, x1200
1280x720 (4 Mbps)	29.97P	x0.5

* The playback bit rate will change automatically to 90 Mbps.

(i) NOTES

• Slow & fast motion recording cannot be used together with the following functions.
   - Dual recording   - Pre-recording
   - Relay recording   - Color bars
• When the slow motion rate is set to x0.5 (59.94P), x0.25 (29.97P) or x0.2 (23.98P), face detection & tracking cannot be used together with slow & fast motion recording.
• About the time code when slow & fast motion recording is activated:
   - The time code mode can be set to [REGEN Regen.], or to [PRESET Preset] with [RECRUN Rec Run] running mode.
   - If the time code running mode was set to [FREERUN Free Run], the time code running mode will be changed automatically to [RECRUN Rec Run] when slow & fast motion recording is activated.
   - When slow & fast motion recording is turned off, the time code running mode will return to its previous setting.
   - The time code signal cannot be output from the HDMI OUT terminal.
• The maximum continuous recording time of a single clip using slow motion recording is the equivalent of 6 hours of playback time. Consequently, it differs depending on the slow motion rate used. For example, when the [x0.5] rate is selected, the maximum continuous recording time will be 3 hours (which, played back at x0.5 slow motion, equal 6 hours of playback time).

Adjusting the Focus

The camcorder offers the following 3 ways to focus. You can also adjust the focus remotely using Browser Remote on a connected network device (□ 111, 117).

Manual focus: Turn the focus/zoom ring to adjust the focus manually. You can use the focus assistance functions (□ 46) to help you focus more accurately when using the manual focus.

AF-Boosted MF: Focus manually most of the way and let the camcorder finish focusing automatically.

Continuous AF: The camcorder continuously focuses on the subject inside the AF frame.

Manual Focus

Use the focus/zoom ring to focus manually. With the ['🎥 Camera Setup] ❯ [Focus Ring Direction] and [Focus Ring Response] settings, you can adjust the direction and responsiveness of the focus/zoom ring when it is used to adjust the focus.

Operating modes: CAMERA | M

1 Set the focus/zoom ring switch to FOCUS.

2 Activate the manual focus.

[FUNC] ❯ [◉ Focus] ❯ [M Manual]

- Alternatively, you can press the AF/MF button to switch between autofocus and manual focus without using the FUNC menu. When **MF** appears on the screen, skip to step 5.

3 You can touch a subject inside the frame to focus on it automatically.

- The Touch AF mark (⁌) will flash and the camcorder will focus automatically. You can then continue to focus manually from the selected point.

- When you adjust the focus, the current approximate focusing distance will appear inside the focus frame.

4 Touch [✕].

5 Turn the focus/zoom ring to focus.

Focus/zoom ring

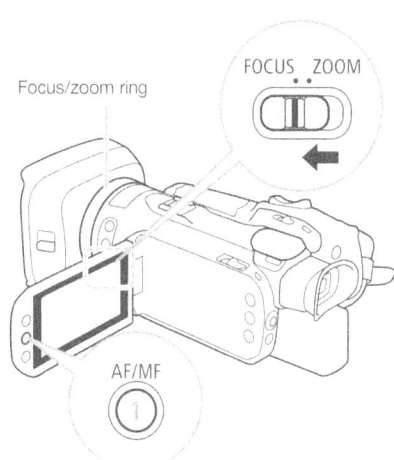

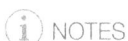

(i) NOTES

- If you operate the zoom after focusing, the focus on the subject may be lost.
- If you focus manually and then leave the camcorder with the power turned on, the focus on the subject may be lost after a while. This possible slight shift in focus is a result of the internal temperature rising. Check the focus before resuming shooting.

Focus Preset

When manual focus is activated, you can register a certain focus point and then, after you focus manually somewhere else, have the camcorder return to the preset focus position. With the ['🎥 Camera Setup] ❯ [Focus Preset Speed] setting, you can set the speed at which the camcorder returns to the preset focus position to one of three levels.

1 Activate the manual focus using the FUNC menu and adjust the focus to the desired position (🕮 45).
   • The current approximate focusing distance will appear inside the focus frame and in the focus preset button.

2 Touch the focus preset button to save the current focus position.
   • The indicator inside the button will turn orange to show the focus preset function was activated.
   • Touch the focus preset button again to turn off the focus preset function.

3 Adjust the focus as necessary using touch AF or the focus/zoom ring.
   • The current focusing distance will appear inside the focus frame.

4 Touch [PRESET] to return to the preset focus position.
   • [PRESET] will be grayed out while adjusting the focus or zoom.

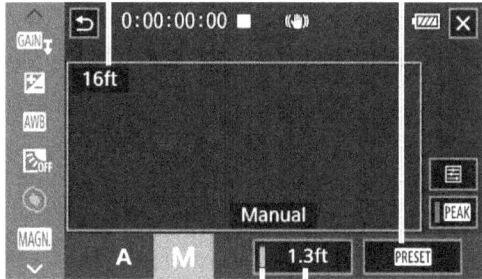

Current focusing distance   Touch to return to the preset focus position

Focus preset button (in orange: focus preset activated)   Preset focus position

(i) NOTES

• The preset focus position will be canceled when the camcorder is turned off.
• Focusing distances are approximate. You can change the distance units used with the [🖵 Display Setup] ❯ [Distance Units] setting.

Using the Focus Assistance Functions

In order to focus more accurately, you can use the following focus assistance functions: Dual Pixel Focus Guide, an onscreen guide that shows you if the subject is in focus; peaking, which creates a clearer contrast by emphasizing the outlines of the subject; and magnification, which enlarges the image on the screen. You can use peaking and the focus guide or peaking and magnification simultaneously for greater effect.

Dual Pixel Focus Guide

The focus guide gives you an intuitive visual indication of the current focus distance and the direction and amount of adjustment necessary to bring the picture into full focus. When used in combination with face detection and tracking (🕮 50), the guide will focus on the vicinity of the eyes of the person detected as the main subject.

By default, the focus guide is activated. If it was turned off, start the procedure from step 1 to activate it.

1 Activate the focus guide.
   MENU ❯ ['🎥 [2] Camera Setup] ❯ [Focus Guide] ❯ [ON On] ❯ [✕]
   • The focus guide will appear on the screen.

2 If necessary, move the focus guide to a different subject you wish to focus on.
   • Touch the desired area on the LCD screen to move the focus guide.

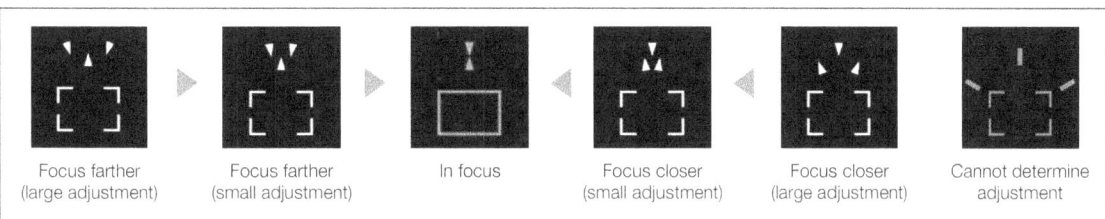

| Focus farther (large adjustment) | Focus farther (small adjustment) | In focus | Focus closer (small adjustment) | Focus closer (large adjustment) | Cannot determine adjustment |

(i) NOTES

- With subjects or in situations where autofocus may not work well (□ 50), the focus guide may not work correctly.
- The Dual Pixel Focus Guide function cannot be used in the following cases:
  - While the focus is being adjusted automatically using AF-boosted MF or continuous AF.
  - When ['🎥 Camera Setup] ❯ [Conversion Lens] is set to an option other than [**OFF** Off].
  - When the digital zoom is activated and the zoom ratio is in the digital zoom range.
  - When the shooting mode is set to ✳.
  - While the color bars are displayed.
- When the Dual Pixel Focus Guide function is used together with face detection & tracking, the focus guide may not focus the main subject's eyes correctly, depending on the direction in which the face is turned.
- If you set an assignable button to [⌁ Focus Guide] (□ 86), you can press the button to turn focus guide on/off.

Peaking

When peaking is activated, the edges of objects in focus will be highlighted in red, blue or yellow on the screen. In addition, you can choose to switch the screen to black & white while peaking is activated, further emphasizing the edges.

1 Activate the manual focus using the FUNC menu (step 2, □ 45).

2 If necessary, change the peaking settings.

   [亖] ❯ Desired options ❯ [⤺]

   - For the black & white setting: Touch [Off] or [On]. For the peaking color: Touch [Red], [Blue] or [Yellow].

3 Touch [**PEAK**] and then touch [✕].

   - Peaking is activated and edges are highlighted.
   - Touch [**PEAK**] again (before closing the menu) to turn off the peaking effect.

Magnification

1 Press the MAGN. button.

- **MAGN.** appears at the lower right of the screen and the center of the screen* is magnified 2 times.
- The frame displayed at the bottom right corner of the screen (magnification frame) shows the approximate part of the image shown magnified.

2 If necessary, move around the magnification frame to check other parts of the image.

- Drag your finger on the LCD screen or push the joystick (▲▼ ◄►).

3 Press the MAGN. button again or touch [✖] to cancel the magnification.

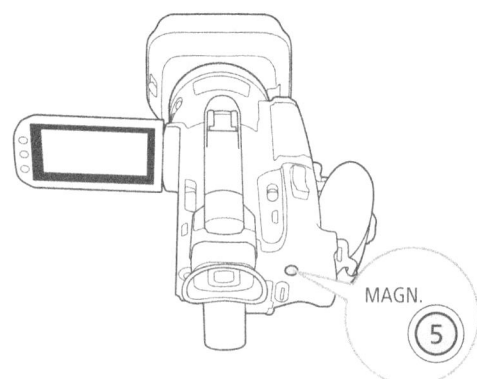

MAGN.
(5)

* If one of the AF frames or a face detection frame is displayed on the screen, the area around the active frame will be magnified instead.

(i) NOTES

- About peaking/magnification:
  - The assistance functions are only displayed on the camcorder's screen. They will not appear on video output from the output terminals and will not affect your recordings.
  - Magnification is not available while the color bars are displayed.

AF-Boosted MF

With this focus mode, you can focus manually most of the way and let the camcorder finish focusing automatically. This is very convenient when you want to make certain that your 4K recordings are in sharp focus. Additionally, with this mode, if the camcorder cannot evaluate how to adjust the focus, it will not perform unreliable focus adjustments. This results in an overall smoother focusing operation than with continuous AF.

Operating modes: CAMERA | M

1 Set the focus/zoom ring to FOCUS.

2 M mode only: Press the AF/MF button to activate the autofocus.

- AF will appear at the left of the screen.

3 Change the AF frame size to [L Large] or [S Small] (□ 49).

4 Set the AF mode to [BOOST AF-Boosted MF].

MENU ❯ ['♛ 1 Camera Setup] ❯ [AF Mode] ❯ BOOST AF-Boosted MF] ❯ [✖]

- When the focus is in the manual adjustment range, a yellow AF frame will appear on the screen.
- If necessary, touch the desired area on the LCD screen to move the AF frame. You can also change the size of the AF frame (□ 49).

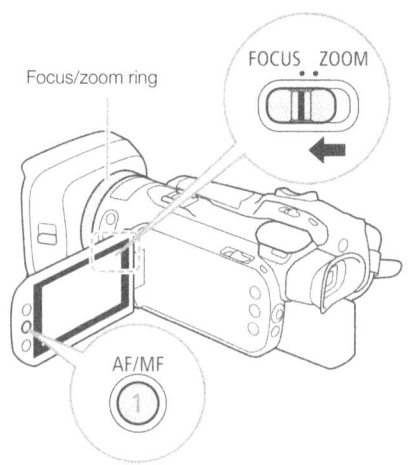

FOCUS   ZOOM

Focus/zoom ring

AF/MF
(1)

5 Turn the focus/zoom ring to adjust the focus.
- Focus manually to bring the subject closer into focus. When the focus enters the automatic adjustment range, the AF frame will turn white and the camcorder will then finish focusing automatically.
- While the focus stays within the automatic adjustment range, the camcorder will keep the subject in focus automatically.

Continuous AF

By default, the camcorder will focus automatically on a subject at the center of the screen. If the AF frame size has been changed to an option other than [**A** Automatic] (□ 49), the camcorder will focus automatically on a subject inside the AF frame that appears on the screen.

Operating modes: 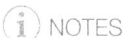 | AUTO M

1 M mode only: Press the AF/MF button to activate the autofocus.
- AF will appear at the left of the screen.
2 Set the AF mode to [CONT Continuous].
MENU ❯ ['🎥 ① Camera Setup] ❯ [AF Mode] ❯
[CONT Continuous] ❯ [✕]

ⓘ NOTES
- When ['🎥 Camera Setup] ❯ [AF Frame Size] is set to [L Large] or [S Small], a white AF frame will appear on the screen.

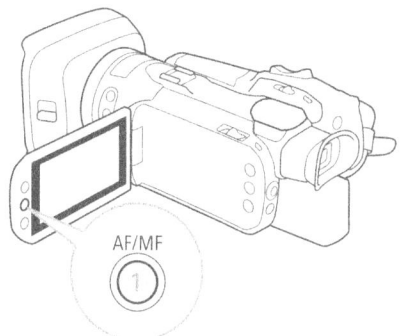

Changing the AF Frame Size

By default, the camcorder focuses on a subject at the center of the screen. You can change the size of the AF frame to display an AF frame and select a specific area (or subject) for autofocus functions. To move the AF frame, simply touch the desired area on the LCD screen.

Operating modes: CAMERA | AUTO M

1 Select [AF Frame Size].
MENU ❯ ['🎥 ② Camera Setup] ❯ [AF Frame Size]
2 Touch the desired option and then touch [✕].

Options
[**A** Automatic]: No AF frame is displayed. The camcorder focuses automatically on a subject at the center of the screen.
[L Large], [S Small]:
An AF frame is displayed and can be moved to focus on a specific subject within an area of about 80% of the screen. You can select the size of the AF frame according to the subject on which you want to focus.

(i) NOTES

• When the AF frame size is set to [**A** Automatic], AF-Boosted MF cannot be used.

About the autofocus (AF) functions:

• You can change some aspects of the autofocus function with the following settings.

- ['🎥 Camera Setup] ❯ [AF Speed] to set the AF speed (the speed at which the focus is adjusted) to one of 3 levels.

- ['🎥 Camera Setup] ❯ [AF Response] to set the responsiveness of the autofocus function to one of 3 levels.

• When recording in bright surroundings, the camcorder closes down the aperture. This may cause the picture to appear blurred and is more noticeable toward the wide angle end of the zoom range. In such case, in [**M**] mode, you can set the shooting mode to **Av** or **M**, apply the ND filter and adjust the aperture.

• Autofocus is not available when ['🎥 Camera Setup] ❯ [Conversion Lens] is set to a setting other than [**OFF** Off].

• Autofocus takes longer to focus when the frame rate is set to 29.97P or 23.98P.

• When recording under dark conditions, the focusing range narrows and the picture may appear blurred.

• While using autofocus, you can turn the focus/zoom ring to focus manually. When you stop turning the ring, the camcorder returns to autofocus. This is useful in situations such as when focusing on a subject on the other side of a window.

• When the shooting mode is set to ❋, the focus will be set to ∞ and cannot be changed.

• Autofocus may not work well on the following subjects or in the following cases. In such case, focus manually.

- Reflective surfaces
- Subjects with low contrast or without vertical lines
- Fast moving subjects
- When [FUNC] ❯ [Looks] is set to [❀2 Wide DR].
- When subjects at different distances appear inside the AF frame.

- Through dirty or wet windows
- Night scenes
- Subjects with a repetitive pattern

Face Detection & Tracking

When face detection & tracking is activated and the camcorder detects a face, it can automatically adjust the focus and exposure* for that person (main subject). When multiple faces are detected, you can touch a different face to make it the main subject. In autofocus mode, you can even track moving subjects other than people (for example, a pet). To select the subject, you will need to use the touch screen.

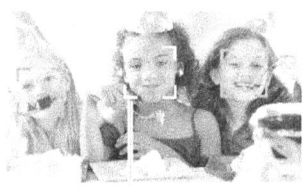

Main subject

* The exposure is not adjusted when the shooting mode is set to **M** or to a Special Scene mode other than ❀ or ❀.

By default, the face detection & tracking function is activated. If it was turned off, start the procedure from step 1 to activate it. In [AUTO] mode, face detection & tracking is always activated and cannot be turned off.

Operating modes: [CAMERA] | [AUTO] [M]

1 Activate face detection & tracking.

MENU ❯ ['🎥 ② Camera Setup] ❯ [Face Detection & Tracking] ❯ [**ON** On 😐] ❯ [✕]

• 😐 will appear at the left of the screen.

2 Point the camcorder at the subject.

• In AF mode, a white frame with small arrows will appear around the main subject. Other faces will have gray frames.

• In MF mode, all faces will have gray frames and the main subject will be indicated with small arrows.

3 If necessary, touch the desired subject on the LCD screen to select a different main subject.

- **To select a different person:** Touch a face with a gray frame. The face detection frame will change to a double frame ⌜⌝ (tracking frame, white in AF mode, gray in MF mode). The camcorder will track the subject as it moves.
- **To select other moving subjects:** In autofocus mode only, you can touch [⌜⌝] and then touch any other moving subject, such as a pet. The frame will change to a white double frame ⌜⌝ (tracking frame). The camcorder will track the subject as it moves.
- Touch [⌜⌝OFF] to remove the frame and cancel the tracking.

4 In manual focus mode, the focus guide will appear on the selected main subject if this function is activated. Use the focus guide as a reference to focus manually.

- In autofocus mode, the camcorder will keep the focus on the main subject and track it as it moves.

Limiting Autofocus to Faces

While using autofocus, you can limit the autofocus function only to cases when a face is detected and use manual focus otherwise. When a face is detected, the camcorder will automatically keep the subject in focus and optimize the exposure.

Operating modes: CAMERA | M

Set an assignable button to [Face Only AF] (86) and press the button.

- While face-only AF is activated, the 🙂 icon will change to 🙂.

(i) NOTES

- The camcorder may mistakenly detect the faces of non-human subjects. In such case, turn face detection & tracking off.
- When face detection is activated, the slowest shutter speed used by the camcorder is 1/30 (1/24 if the frame rate is set to 23.98P).
- Touching somewhere with a color or pattern unique to the subject will make it easier to track. However, if there is another subject in the vicinity that shares similar characteristics to the selected subject, the camcorder may start tracking the incorrect subject. Select the desired subject using the "To select other moving subjects" procedure (step 3, 50).
- In certain cases, faces may not be detected correctly. Typical examples include:
  - Faces extremely small, large, dark or bright in relation to the overall picture.
  - Faces turned to the side, upside down, at a diagonal or partially hidden.
- Face detection & tracking cannot be used in the following cases.
  - When the shooting mode is set to , or .
  - When the shutter speed used is slower than 1/30 (1/24 if the frame rate is set to 23.98P).
  - When the digital zoom is activated and the zoom ratio is larger than 60x.
  - When slow & fast motion recording is activated and the slow motion rate is set to x0.5 (59.94P), x0.25 (29.97P) or x0.2 (23.98P).
- In certain cases, the camcorder may not be able to track the subject. Typical examples include:
  - Subjects extremely small or large in relation to the overall picture.
  - Subjects too similar to the background.
  - Subjects lacking sufficient contrast.
  - Fast moving subjects.
  - When shooting indoors with insufficient lighting.

Zooming

To zoom in and out, you can use the focus/zoom ring, the zoom rocker on the camcorder, the zoom buttons on the wireless controller or the onscreen zoom controls. You can also zoom using Browser Remote on a connected network device (◻ 111, 117).

In addition to the 15x optical zoom, in [M] mode, you can turn on the digital zoom* (300x) with the ['🎥 Camera Setup] ❯ [Digital Zoom] setting. The camcorder also features a digital tele-converter, which allows you to enlarge the image on the screen digitally.

* Digital zoom is not available in [AUTO] mode or when ['🎥 Camera Setup] ❯ [Conversion Lens] is set to [**Wide** WA-U58].

Operating modes: 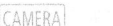 |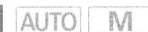

Using the Focus/Zoom Ring

1 Set the focus/zoom ring switch to ZOOM.

2 Turn the focus/zoom ring to adjust the zoom.

- Turn the focus/zoom ring slowly for a slow zoom; turn it faster for faster zooms.

- The zoom bar that appears on the screen indicates the approximate zoom position.

(i) NOTES

- With the ['🎥 Camera Setup] ❯ [Zoom Ring Direction] setting, you can adjust the direction of the focus/zoom ring when it is used to adjust the zoom.

- If you turn the focus/zoom ring too quickly, the camcorder may not be able to zoom immediately. In such case, the camcorder will zoom after you finish turning the ring.

Focus/zoom ring

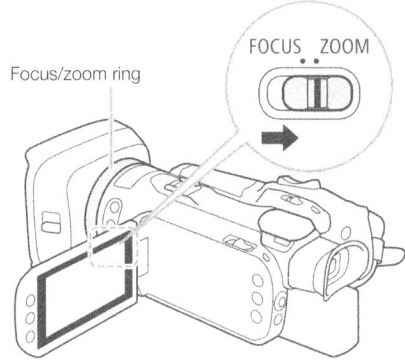

Using the Zoom Rocker

Move the zoom rocker toward **W** (wide angle) to zoom out.
Move it toward **T** (telephoto) to zoom in.

- By default, the zoom rocker operates at a variable speed. You can also set it to a constant speed and select the zoom speed.

Setting the Zoom Speed

Refer to the following table for approximate zoom speeds.

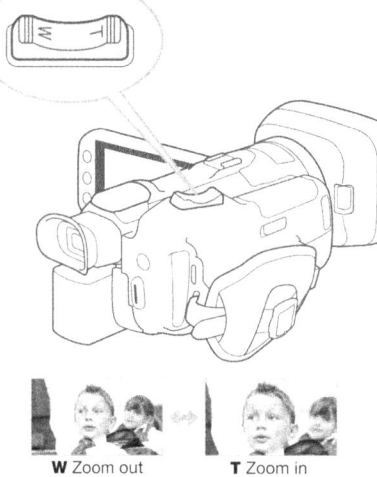

W Zoom out   **T** Zoom in

Camcorder's zoom rocker: Approximate zoom speeds (time required to zoom end-to-end)

[Zoom Rocker Zoom Speed] setting	Selected constant speed	[Zoom Speed Level] setting		
		[▶ Slow]	[▶▶ Normal]	[▶▶▶ Fast]*
[VAR] (variable)	–	4.2 sec. to 4 min. 38 sec.	2.6 sec. to 2 min.	1.5 sec. to 1 min.
[CONST] (constant)	1 (slowest)	4 min. 38 sec.	2 min.	1 min.
	16 (fastest)	4.2 sec.	2.6 sec.	1.5 sec.

* When the zoom speed is too fast, the camcorder may have more trouble focusing automatically while zooming.

1 Select the overall zoom speed level.

MENU ❯ ['🎥 ① Camera Setup] ❯ [Zoom Speed Level] ❯ Desired zoom speed level ❯ [↩]

- You can select one of three levels, [▶▶▶ Fast], [▶▶ Normal] or [▶ Slow].

2 Select whether to use a variable or constant zoom speed.

[Zoom Rocker Zoom Speed] ❯ [VAR] (variable) or [CONST] (constant)

- If you selected [VAR], skip to step 4.

3 Touch [◀] or [▶], or drag your finger along the adjustment bar, to set the desired constant speed.

4 Touch [✕].

(i) NOTES

- When [Zoom Speed Level] is set to [▶▶▶ Fast], the camcorder may pick up and record lens operations sounds.

To use high-speed zoom in standby mode

When high-speed zoom is activated and ['🎥 Camera Setup] ❯ [Zoom Rocker Zoom Speed] is set to [**VAR**] (variable zoom speed), in record standby mode you will be able to zoom at the highest speed available ([**▶▶** Fast]). Nevertheless, the zoom speed while recording will be determined by the [Zoom Speed Level] setting.

1 Select [High-Speed Zoom].

MENU ❯ ['🎥 ① Camera Setup] ❯ [High-Speed Zoom]

2 Touch [**ON** On] and then touch [✖].

ⓘ NOTES

• When pre-recording is activated, the zoom speed will be determined by the [Zoom Speed Level] setting even in record standby mode.

Using the Supplied Wireless Controller or an Optional Remote Controller

The zoom speeds when using the supplied wireless controller, the optional RC-V100 Remote Controller or a commercially available remote control connected to the REMOTE terminal are different.
You can also zoom remotely using Browser Remote on a connected network device (🔲 111, 117).

Zoom speeds for remote operation

Accessory	Zoom speed
Wireless controller (supplied)	Constant zoom speed. See the following table.
RC-V100 Remote Controller (optional)	Variable speed: The greater the angle at which the RC-V100's ZOOM dial is rotated from the center, the faster the zoom.
Commercially available remote controls	If the remote control does not support variable zoom: Constant zoom speed. If the remote control supports variable zoom: Variable zoom according to the remote control's settings.

Wireless controller: Approximate zoom speeds (time required to zoom end-to-end)

[Wireless Ctrlr Zoom Speed] setting	[Zoom Speed Level] setting		
	[**▶** Slow]	[**▶▶** Normal]	[**▶▶** Fast]*
1 (slowest)	4 min. 38 sec.	2 min.	1 min.
16 (fastest)	4.2 sec.	2.6 sec.	1.5 sec.

* When the zoom speed is too fast, the camcorder may have more trouble focusing automatically while zooming.

1 Select the overall zoom speed level (step 1, 🔲 53).

2 Select [Wireless Ctrlr Zoom Speed].

3 Touch [◀] or [▶], or drag your finger along the adjustment bar, to set the desired constant speed.

4 Touch [✖].

ⓘ NOTES

• When an optional RC-V100 Remote Controller is connected to the camcorder, you can zoom with the remote controller's ZOOM dial. At default settings, turn the dial right to zoom in (**T**) and left to zoom out (**W**).

Using the Touch Screen's Zoom Controls

1 Open the onscreen zoom controls.

[FUNC] ❯❯ [ZOOM Zoom]

- The zoom controls appear at the bottom the screen.

2 Touch the zoom controls to operate the zoom.

- Touch anywhere within the **W** area to zoom out or anywhere within the **T** area to zoom in. Touch closer to the center for a slow zoom; touch closer to the **W**/**T** icons for faster zooms.

3 Touch [**✕**].

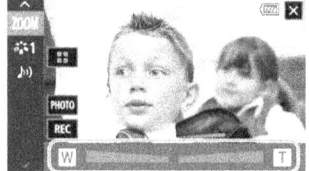

Digital Tele-Converter

Using the digital tele-converter, you can digitally increase the focal length of the camcorder by a factor of approx. 2 and record the enlarged image.

Operating modes: [CAMERA] | [M]

1 Enable the use of the digital tele-converter function.

MENU ❯❯ ['🎥 ① Camera Setup] ❯❯ [Digital Zoom] ❯❯ [2.0x Digital Tele-conv.] ❯❯ [**✕**]

2 Open the onscreen zoom controls.

[FUNC] ❯❯ [ZOOM Zoom]

3 Touch [2.0x] (digital tele-converter) and then touch [**✕**].

- The center of the screen will be enlarged approximately 2 times and the 2.0x icon will appear at the lower left of the screen.

- Touch [2.0x] again (before closing the screen) to turn off the digital tele-converter.

(ⓘ) NOTES

- You can attach the optional TL-U58 Tele-converter and use it in conjunction with this function to increase the effect.

- The digital tele-converter cannot be activated while recording or when ['🎥 Camera Setup] ❯❯ [Conversion Lens] is set to [Wide WA-U58].

- The image is digitally processed so the image will deteriorate throughout the zoom range.

Image Stabilization

Use the image stabilizer to compensate for camcorder shake in order to achieve steadier shots. The camcorder offers 3 methods of image stabilization.

Dynamic IS ((❰❱)): Dynamic IS compensates for a higher degree of camcorder shake, such as when shooting while walking, and is more effective as the zoom approaches full wide angle.

Standard IS ((❰❱)): Standard IS compensates for a lower degree of camcorder shake, for example, for handheld shots while you remain stationary, and is suitable for shooting natural-looking scenes.

Powered IS (❰❱): Powered IS is most effective when you are stationary and zooming in on far subjects using high zoom ratios (the more you approach the telephoto end). This mode is not suitable for tilting and panning shots.

Operating modes: [CAMERA] | [AUTO] [M]

Dynamic IS or Standard IS

1 Select [Image Stabilizer].

MENU ❭ ['🎥 ③ Camera Setup] ❭ [Image Stabilizer]

2 Touch [(❰❱) Standard] (Standard IS) or [(❰❱) Dynamic] (Dynamic IS) and then touch [✕].
   • Touch [(❰❱) Off] instead to turn off the image stabilization, for example, when the camcorder is mounted on a tripod.
   • The icon of the selected mode appears at the top center of the screen.

Powered IS

Press and hold the POWERED IS button as long as you want to activate Powered IS.
   • (❰❱) appears in yellow while Powered IS is activated.

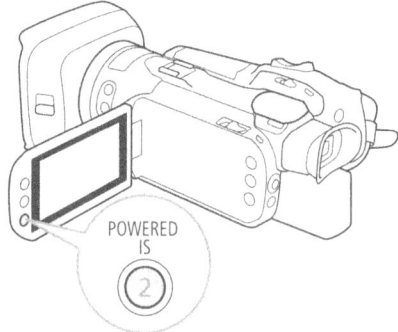

(i) NOTES
   • The angle of view will change when [Image Stabilizer] is set to [(❰❱) Dynamic].
   • If the degree of camcorder shake is too high, the image stabilizer may not be able to compensate fully.
   • Powered IS is available even when [Image Stabilizer] is set to [(❰❱) Off].
   • You can change the operation of the POWERED IS button (long press or toggle on/off) with the ['🎥 Camera Setup] ❭ [Powered IS Button] setting.
   • When using Dynamic IS, the edges of the picture may be adversely affected (ghosting, artifacts and/or dark areas may appear) when compensating for a high degree of camcorder shake.

Automatic Gain Control (AGC) Limit

When recording in dark surroundings, the camcorder will automatically increase the gain to try to get a brighter picture. By setting a maximum gain value, you can limit the amount of noise in the picture and keep a darker look. This function can only be used when the shooting mode is set to **P**, **Tv** or **Av**.

Operating modes: [CAMERA] | [M]

1 Open the AGC limit adjustment screen.

[FUNC] ❯ [[GAIN] AGC Limit] ❯ [**M**]

- An adjustment dial will appear on the screen.
- Touch [**M**] again to return the camcorder to automatic gain control.

2 Touch [◀] or [▶], or drag your finger along the dial, to set the desired maximum gain value.

- You can select an AGC limit from 0.0 dB to 38.0 dB.
- If [FUNC] ❯ [Looks] is set to [✿2 Wide DR], the lowest AGC limit that can be set will be 9.0 dB.

3 Touch [✕].

- When an AGC limit is set, [GAIN] and the maximum gain value will appear at the left of the screen.

(i) NOTES

- The AGC limit cannot be set when the exposure is locked (□ 61).
- If you set [✿ System Setup] ❯ [CUSTOM Dial & Button] to [[GAIN] AGC Limit] (□ 85), you can adjust the AGC limit with the CUSTOM dial and button.

Shooting Modes

This camcorder offers a number of shooting modes that give you varying degrees of control over the camcorder's settings. Select the shooting mode most appropriate to your needs or creative vision and adjust manually those settings you wish to control, letting the camcorder take care of the rest.

You can also change the shooting mode remotely using Browser Remote on a connected network device (□ 111, 116).

Operating modes: CAMERA | M

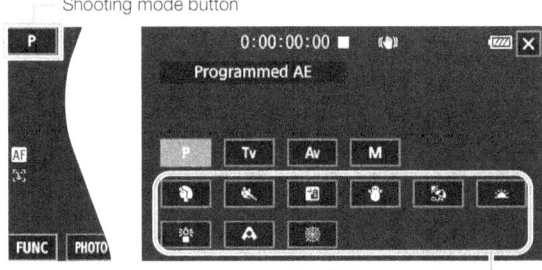

Shooting mode button

Special Scene modes

1 Touch the shooting mode button.

2 Touch the desired shooting mode and then touch [✕].

 • The shooting mode button will show the selected mode's icon.

Programmed AE (P)

The camcorder automatically sets the shutter speed, aperture and gain (for clips) but you will have the option to use other functions that are not available in AUTO mode.

Set the shooting mode to [P Programmed AE].

Shutter Priority AE (Tv)

With this shooting mode you set the shutter speed manually, for example, to capture fast-moving subjects in sharp focus or to obtain a brighter image in low-light situations. The camcorder will automatically adjust other settings to obtain the best exposure.

1 Set the shooting mode to [Tv Shutter-Pri. AE] (□ 58).

 • The shutter speed will appear at the left of the screen.

2 Open the shutter speed screen.

[FUNC] ❯ [SHTR Shutter Speed]

 • An adjustment dial will appear on the screen.

 • You can touch [🚫] to display the zebra pattern (□ 63, step 2) and check for overexposed areas.

3 Touch [◀] or [▶], or drag your finger along the dial, to set the desired shutter speed.

 • You can also adjust the shutter speed using the CUSTOM dial (□ 85) or Browser Remote on a connected network device (□ 111, 116).

 • For available shutter speeds, see the manual exposure table (□ 59)

58

Aperture Priority AE (Av)

With this shooting mode you set the aperture value manually to control the depth of field, for example, in order to defocus the background and make the subject stand out more. The camcorder will automatically adjust other settings to obtain the best exposure.

1 Set the shooting mode to [Av Aperture-Pri. AE] (□ 58).
  - The aperture value will appear at the left of the screen.

2 Open the aperture screen.

  [FUNC] ❯ [IRIS Aperture]
  - An adjustment dial will appear on the screen.
  - You can touch [⃠] to display the zebra pattern (□ 63, step 2) and check for overexposed areas.

3 Touch [◀] or [▶], or drag your finger along the dial, to set the desired aperture value.
  - You can also adjust the aperture value using the CUSTOM dial (□ 85) or Browser Remote on a connected network device (□ 111, 116).
  - For available aperture values, see the manual exposure table (□ 59)

(i) NOTES

- When the shooting mode is set to Tv or Av, depending on the brightness of the subject, the camcorder may not be able to set the appropriate exposure. In such case the shutter speed (Tv) or aperture value (Av) will flash on the screen. Change the aperture/shutter speed as necessary.

Manual Exposure (M)

This shooting mode gives you the most control over shooting settings as you can set the aperture, shutter speed and gain to get the exposure that you want.

1 Set the shooting mode to [M Manual Exposure] (□ 58).
  - The aperture value, shutter speed and gain value will appear at the left of the screen.

2 Set the aperture and shutter speed as described previously.

  Aperture: [FUNC] ❯ [IRIS Aperture] (□ 59, from step 2)

  Shutter speed: [FUNC] ❯ [SHTR Shutter Speed] (□ 58, from step 2)

3 Open the gain screen.

  [FUNC] ❯ [GAIN Gain]
  - An adjustment dial will appear on the screen.
  - You can touch [⃠] to display the zebra pattern (□ 63, step 2) and check for overexposed areas.

4 Touch [◀] or [▶], or drag your finger along the dial, to set the desired gain value.
  - You can also adjust the gain value using the CUSTOM dial (□ 85) or Browser Remote on a connected network device (□ 111, 116).

Available settings

The following aperture values, shutter speeds and gain values are available in the various shooting modes.

Aperture*	F2.8, F3.2, F3.4, F3.7, F4.0, F4.4, F4.8, F5.2, F5.6, F6.2, F6.7, F7.3, F8.0, F8.7, F9.5, F10, F11
Shutter speed	1/6**, 1/8, 1/9, 1/10, 1/12, 1/15, 1/17, 1/20, 1/24, 1/25, 1/30, 1/34, 1/40, 1/48, 1/50, 1/60, 1/75, 1/90, 1/100, 1/120, 1/150, 1/180, 1/210, 1/250, 1/300, 1/360, 1/420, 1/500, 1/600, 1/720, 1/840, 1/1000, 1/1200, 1/1400, 1/1700, 1/2000
Gain	0.0 dB*** to 39.0 dB (1-dB increments)

* Aperture values displayed on the screen are for reference only.
** Only when the frame rate is 23.98P.
*** From 9.0 dB when [FUNC] ❯ [Looks] is set to [✳2 Wide DR].

The exposure bar

When the shooting mode is set to **M**, the exposure bar will appear on the screen, showing the optimal automatic exposure and current exposure. When the difference between current and optimal exposure is larger than ±2 EV, the indicator will flash at the edge of the exposure bar.

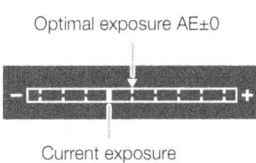

Optimal exposure AE±0

Current exposure

Special Scene Modes

The Special Scene shooting modes offer preset combinations of settings optimized for specific situations. Using a Special Scene mode can be an easy and convenient alternative to adjusting detailed exposure settings.

Set the shooting mode to the desired Special Scene shooting mode (□ 58).

[Portrait]
The camcorder uses a large aperture, to achieve a sharp focus on the subject while blurring the background.

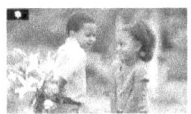

[Sunset]
To record sunsets in vibrant colors.

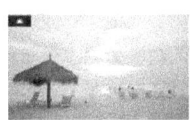

[Sports]
To record sports scenes, such as sporting events or dance scenes.

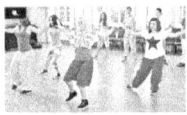

[Low Light]
To record in low-light situations.

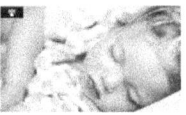

[Night Scene]
To record nightscapes with lower noise.

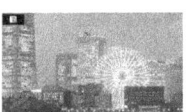

[Spotlight]
To record spotlit scenes.

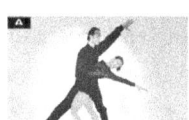

[Snow]
To record in bright ski resorts without the subject being underexposed.

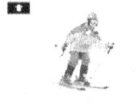

[Fireworks]
To record fireworks.

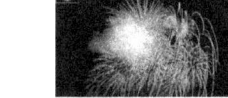

[Beach]
To record on a sunny beach without the subject being underexposed.

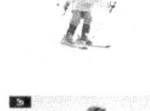

(i) NOTES

• [Portrait]/[Sports]/[Snow]/[Beach]: The picture may not appear smooth during playback.
• [Snow]/[Beach]: The subject may become overexposed on cloudy days or in shaded places. Check the image on the screen.
• [Low Light]:
  - Moving subjects may leave a trailing afterimage.
  - Picture quality may not be as good as in other modes.
  - White points may appear on the screen.
  - Autofocus may not work as well as in other modes. In such case, adjust the focus manually.
• [Low Light]/[Fireworks]: To avoid camcorder blur (blur due to the camcorder moving) we recommend using a tripod.

Adjusting the Exposure

At times, the overall exposure obtained automatically by the camcorder may not be best for a specific subject or for parts of the image. The following exposure-related functions can help you achieve the desired brightness. You can also adjust the exposure remotely using Browser Remote on a connected network device (□ 111, 116).

Operating modes: [CAMERA] | [M]

Exposure Lock (AE Lock)

You can lock the current exposure settings and use them even when you reframe the picture. This function can only be used when the shooting mode is set to **P**, **Tv**, **Av** or one of the Special Scene modes, except for [⚬ Fireworks].

1 Open the exposure screen.

[FUNC] ❯ [☒ Exposure Comp.]

- An adjustment dial will appear on the screen.
- You can touch [▨] to display the zebra pattern (□ 63, step 2) and check for overexposed areas.

2 Touch [☀] to lock the current exposure.

- Touch [☀] again to return the camcorder to automatic exposure.

3 Touch [◀] or [▶], or drag your finger along the dial, to further compensate the exposure.

- Depending on the brightness of the image and the exposure locked, some values may not be available and the available exposure compensation range may differ.

4 Touch [✕].

- The exposure value that was locked and ☀ will appear in orange at the left of the screen.

Touch Exposure

You can touch the screen to optimize the exposure for a specific subject or area. The camcorder will automatically adjust the exposure for the selected point and lock the exposure settings. You can even touch a bright area of the image to try to avoid overexposure (Highlight AE). This function can only be used when the shooting mode is set to **P**, **Tv**, **Av** or one of the Special Scene modes, except for [⚬ Fireworks].

1 Open the exposure screen.

[FUNC] ❯ [☒ Exposure Comp.]

- An adjustment dial will appear on the screen.
- You can touch [▨] to display the zebra pattern (□ 63, step 2) and check for overexposed areas.

2 To use the Highlight AE function, change the touch exposure settings.

[☰] ❯ [Ⓗ Highlights] ❯ [↩]

3 Touch the desired area on the LCD screen to optimize and lock the exposure.

- The ⚬ mark will flash and the exposure will be adjusted automatically so the area you touched will be correctly exposed.

4 Touch [✕].

- The exposure value that was locked and ☀ will appear in orange at the left of the screen.
- Instead of touching [✕], you can continue from step 2 in the following procedure to further compensate the exposure.

(i) NOTES

- The camcorder will return to automatic exposure in the following cases.
  - When the camcorder is turned off.
  - When the operating mode, shooting mode or frame rate is changed.
  - When [FUNC] ❯ [Looks] is switched between [❊2 Wide DR] and one of the other settings or vice versa.

Exposure Compensation

You can compensate the exposure that was set using automatic aperture, in order to darken or lighten the image.
This function can only be used when the shooting mode is set to P, Tv or Av.

1 Open the exposure screen.

[FUNC] ❯ [☒ Exposure Comp.]

- If the exposure was locked, touch [✳] to unlock the automatic exposure.
- An adjustment dial will appear on the screen.
- You can touch [⊿⁄̶ₒₓₓ] to display the zebra pattern (□ 63, step 2) and check for overexposed areas.

2 Touch [◀] or [▶], or drag your finger along the dial, to compensate the exposure.

- You can select one of 17 exposure compensation levels from −2 to +2.

3 Touch [✖].

- [AE] and the exposure compensation value will appear in orange at the left of the screen.

(i) NOTES

- If you set [♀ System Setup] ❯ [CUSTOM Dial & Button] to [☒ Exposure Comp.] (□ 85), you can compensate the exposure with the CUSTOM dial and button.

Backlight Correction

When you need to record a scene with constant backlight conditions, you can use backlight correction to make the picture, especially the darker areas, brighter.
This function cannot be used when the shooting mode is set to ❋.

1 Select [☒ₒₓₓ BLC Always On].

[FUNC] ❯ [☒ₒₓₓ BLC Always On]

2 Touch [☒ On] and then touch [✖].

- ☒ will appear at the left of the screen.

(i) NOTES

- If you set an assignable button to [☒ BLC Always On] (□ 86), you can press the button to turn the constant backlight correction on and off.
- The camcorder also has an automatic backlight correction function that you can turn on/off with the [🎥 Camera Setup] ❯ [Auto Backlight Correction] setting. The automatic correction can be more convenient when you need to shoot under changing light conditions.

Zebra Pattern

You can use the zebra pattern to identify areas that might be overexposed, so you can correct the exposure appropriately. The camcorder offers two levels of zebra pattern: With 100%, only areas that will lose detail in the highlight areas will be identified, while 70% will identify also areas that are dangerously close to losing detail.

1 Open the exposure screen.

[FUNC] ❯ [☑ Exposure]

2 Select the desired zebra level.

[▨] ❯ [▨ 70%] or [▨ 100%] ❯ [✕]

- To turn off the zebra pattern, touch [▨ Off] instead.
- To return to the exposure screen and change other exposure settings, touch [�] instead of [✕].
- The zebra pattern will appear on the overexposed areas of the picture.

ⓘ NOTES

- Displaying the zebra pattern on the camcorder's screen will not affect your recordings.

ND Filter

Using the ND filter allows you to open up the aperture to obtain a shallower depth of field even when recording in bright surroundings. You can also use the ND filter to avoid the soft focus caused by diffraction when using small apertures. You can select one of 3 density levels.

You can also change the ND filter remotely using Browser Remote on a connected network device ($\square$ 111, 116).

Operating modes: CAMERA | AUTO M

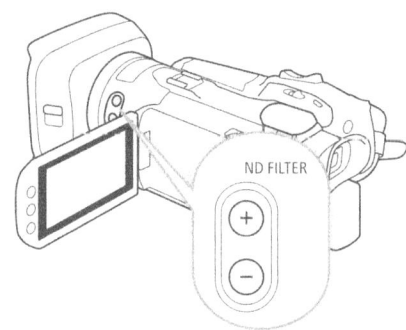

Press the ND FILTER + or – button to select the desired ND filter setting.

- Repeatedly pressing ND FILTER + button will change the ND filter setting in the following order: [ND 1/4] → [ND 1/16] → [ND 1/64] → ND filter off (no onscreen display).
  The ND FILTER – button cycles through the settings in reverse order.
- The selected ND filter setting will appear at the left of the screen.

(i) NOTES

- Depending on the scene, the color may change when turning the ND filter on/off. Setting a custom white balance ($\square$ 65) may be effective in such case.
- **About changing the ND filter setting using the optional RC-V100 Remote Controller:**
  - When the remote controller is connected to the camcorder, you can use the remote controller's ND button in the same way as the camcorder's ND FILTER + button.
  - ND filter indicators 1 to 3 will illuminate in orange when the ND filter is set to 1/4, 1/16 and 1/64, respectively.

White Balance

The white balance function helps you to produce accurate colors under different lighting conditions. This function can only be used when the shooting mode is set to **P**, **Tv**, **Av** or **M**.
You can also adjust the white balance remotely using Browser Remote on a connected network device (📖 111, 116).

Operating modes: CAMERA | M

1 Select [**AWB** White Balance].

[FUNC] ❯ [**AWB** White Balance]

2 Touch the desired option and then touch [✖].

- If you selected [**K** Color Temperature], [Set 1] or [Set 2] and wish to change the color temperature value or register a new custom white balance, continue with the appropriate procedure below instead of touching [✖].
- The icon of the selected option will appear at the left of the screen.

To set the color temperature ([**K** Color Temperature])

3 Touch [⧉].

- An adjustment dial will appear on the screen.

4 Drag your finger along the dial to set the color temperature value.

5 Touch [✖].

To set a custom white balance ([Set 1] or [Set 2])

3 Touch [⧉].

4 Point the camcorder at a gray card or white object so that it fills the frame at the center of the screen and then touch [Set WB].

- When the icon stops flashing, the procedure is completed. The setting is retained even if you turn of f the camcorder.

5 Touch [✖].

Options

[**AWB** Automatic]:   The camcorder automatically sets the white balance for natural looking colors.

[☀ Daylight]:   To record outdoors on a bright day.

[🔆 Tungsten]:   To record under tungsten and tungsten-type (3-wavelength) fluorescent lighting.

[**K** Color Temperature]:
                Allows you to set the color temperature between 2,000 K and 15,000 K.

[Set 1], [Set 2]:
                Use the custom white balance settings to make white subjects appear white under colored lighting.

(i) NOTES

- **When you select a custom white balance:**
  - Set ['🎥 Camera Setup] ❯ [Digital Zoom] to [OFF Off].
  - Readjust the custom white balance if the light source or ND filter setting changes.
  - Very rarely and depending on the light source, 🔳 may keep flashing (it will change to a slow flashing). The result will still be better than with [AWB Automatic].

- Using a custom white balance may provide better results in the following cases:
  - Changing lighting conditions
  - Close-ups
  - Subjects in a single color (sky, sea or forest)
  - Under mercury lamps, certain types of fluorescent lights and LED lights

Using Looks

The camcorder can shoot using looks — combinations of settings that affect the characteristics of the image produced. The camcorder offers a number of preset looks, some of whose settings you can adjust to your preference.

This function can only be used when the shooting mode is set to **P**, **Tv**, **Av** or **M**.

Operating modes: CAMERA | M

1 Open the looks screen.

[FUNC] ❯ [Looks]

2 Touch the desired option.

- To use the preset look as is, skip to step 4.

3 If necessary, adjust the detailed settings.

[☰] ❯ Touch [–] or [+] to adjust the value

- You can also drag your finger along the adjustment bar.
- The sharpness, contrast and color depth can be adjusted as follows:
  [Sharpness]: 0 (softer image) to 7 (sharper image)
  [Contrast]*: –4 (low contrast) to +4 (high contrast)
  [Color Depth]**: –4 (shallower colors) to +4 (richer colors)

4 Touch [✖].

* Not available for [✿2 Wide DR].   ** Not available for [✿3 Monochrome].

Options

[✿1 Standard]:   Standard look for general shooting situations.

[✿2 Wide DR]:   Applies a gamma curve with a wide dynamic range and colors appropriate for this gamma curve.

[✿3 Monochrome]:
                  Produces a black & white picture.

ⓘ NOTES

- When using the [✿2 Wide DR] look, the lowest available gain setting is 9.0 dB. As such, when shooting outdoors in daylight or other bright surroundings, the subject may appear bright because the camcorder cannot achieve the optimal exposure.

67

Setting the Time Code

The camcorder generates a time code signal and records it with the recorded clips. The time code signal can be output from the HDMI OUT terminal.

Depending on the frame rate used, you may be able to select between a drop frame an non-drop frame time code signal (◻ 69). Though the time code display style is different for DF and NDF, in this section the NDF display style is used for simplicity's sake.

Operating modes: CAMERA | AUTO   M

Selecting the Time Code Mode

1 Select [Time Code Mode].

   MENU ❯ [🗖 ② Recording Setup] ❯ [Time Code Mode]

2 Touch the desired option and then touch [✖].

Options

[PRESET Preset]:   The time code starts from an initial value you can select in advance. The default initial time code is 00:00:00:00.
   See the following procedures to select the time code running mode and set the initial time code.

[REGEN. Regen.]:   The camcorder will read the selected SD card and the time code will continue from the last time code recorded on the card. The time code runs only while recording so clips recorded consecutively on the same SD card will have continuous time codes.

Setting the Time Code Running Mode

If you set the time code mode to [PRESET Preset], you can select the time code running mode.

1 Select [Time Code Running Mode].

   MENU ❯ [🗖 ③ Recording Setup] ❯ [Time Code Running Mode]

2 Touch the desired option and then touch [✖].

Options

[RECRUN Rec Run]:   The time code runs only while recording so clips recorded consecutively on the same SD card will have continuous time codes.

[FREERUN Free Run]:The time code starts running the moment you confirm the selection and keeps running regardless of the camcorder's operation.

Setting the Time Code's Initial Value

If you set the running mode to [PRESET Preset], you can set the initial value of the time code.

1 Select [Initial Time Code].

   MENU ❯ [🗖 ③ Recording Setup] ❯ [Initial Time Code]

   • The time code setting screen appears with an orange selection frame indicating the hours.
   • Touch [Reset] to reset the time code to [00:00:00:00] and return to the previous screen. If the running mode is set to [FREERUN Free Run], the time code will be reset the moment you touch the button and keep running continuously from 00:00:00:00.

2 Touch [▲] or [▼] to set the value for the hours and then touch the minutes field to select it.

   • Change the rest of the fields (minutes, seconds, frame) in the same way.

3 After completing all the fields of the time code, touch [OK].

- Touch [Cancel] to close the screen without changing the time code.
- If the running mode is set to [FREERUN Free Run], the time code will start running from the time code entered the moment you touch [OK].

4 Touch [✕].

Selecting Drop Frame or Non-Drop Frame

When the frame rate is set to 59.94P or 29.97P, you can select between a drop frame (DF) or non-drop frame (NDF) time code, depending on how you plan to use your recordings. When the frame rate is set to 23.98P, the time code is set to non-drop frame (NDF) and cannot be changed.

1 Select [DF/NDF].

MENU ❯ [🗗 3 Recording Setup] ❯ [DF/NDF]

2 Select [DF DF] or [NDF NDF] and then touch [✕].

- The time code display will differ depending on the setting. When you select [DF DF], the time code will appear as [00:00:00.00]; when you select [NDF NDF], it will appear as [00:00:00:00].

(i) NOTES

- When the frame rate is set to 23.98P, the frames value in the time code runs from 0 to 23. For other settings, it runs from 0 to 29.
- When slow & fast motion recording is activated, you cannot select the [FREERUN Free Run] running mode. Conversely, when pre-recording is activated, [FREERUN Free Run] is set automatically and cannot be changed.
- When you mix drop frame and non-drop frame time codes, there might be a discontinuity in the time code at the point where the recording starts.
- When slow & fast motion recording is activated, the time code signal cannot be output from the HDMI OUT terminal.
- When the camcorder is set to external recording-only mode, the time code mode cannot be set to [REGEN. Regen.].
- When you are using the [FREERUN Free Run] running mode, the time code will continue running as long as the built-in backup battery has some charge left, even if you disconnect all other power sources. However, this is less accurate than when the camcorder is on.

Setting the User Bit

The user bit display can be selected from the date or the time of recording, or an identification code consisting of 8 characters in the hexadecimal system. There are sixteen possible characters: the numbers 0 to 9 and the letters A to F. The user bit can be output from the HDMI OUT terminal.

Operating modes: [CAMERA] | [AUTO] [M]

Setting an Hexadecimal Code

1 Open the user bit setting screen.

MENU ❯ [🗗 ③ Recording Setup] ❯ [User Bit Type] ❯ [SET Setting] ❯ [☰]

• The user bit setting screen appears with an orange selection frame on the leftmost digit.

• Touch [Reset] to reset the user bit to [00 00 00 00] and return to the previous screen.

2 Touch [▲] or [▼] to set the first character and then touch the field next to it to select it.

• Change the rest of the characters in the same way.

3 After completing all the characters of the user bit, touch [OK].

• Touch [Cancel] to close the screen without changing the user bit.

Using the Date or Time

1 Select [User Bit Type].

MENU ❯ [🗗 ③ Recording Setup] ❯ [User Bit Type]

2 Touch [DATE Date] or [TIME Time] and then touch [✖].

Using the Mini Advanced Shoe

Using the mini advanced shoe, you can attach to the camcorder a range of optional accessories (□ 142) to expand its functionality. For details about how to attach and use the accessories, refer also to the instruction manual of the accessory used.

Operating modes: │ AUTO M

1 Open the mini advanced shoe cover.
2 Attach the optional accessory to the mini advanced shoe.
   • When a compatible accessory is attached to the mini advanced shoe, „𝓢" will appear on the screen.

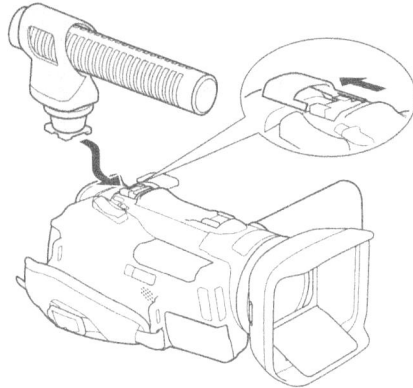

Example: Attaching an optional DM-100 Directional Stereo Microphone.

(i) NOTES

• Accessories designed for the Advanced Accessory Shoe cannot be used with this camcorder. Look for video accessories bearing this logo to ensure compatibility with the **mini advanced shoe**.

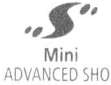

Mini
ADVANCED SHOE

Using an External Video Light

You can use the optional VL-5 Video Light when you need to record movies in dark locations.

Attach the optional video light to the mini advanced shoe.

• „𝓢" will appear on the screen when you turn on the optional video light (ON or AUTO). For details about using the optional video light, refer to the instruction manual of the VL-5.

Recording Audio

The camcorder features 2-channel MPEG-4 AAC-LC audio recording and playback. You can record audio using the built-in microphone, the mini advanced shoe and optional DM-100 Directional Stereo Microphone or the MIC terminal (commercially available microphones).

When recording outdoors in the open, the built-in microphone may record loud audible wind noise. In such cases, using an external microphone with a foam cover or wind screen is recommended.

Operating modes: [CAMERA] | [AUTO] [M]

Using an External Microphone

Using the DM-100 Directional Stereo Microphone you can accurately record audio mainly from the direction where the camcorder is pointing. To reduce wind noise, attach the wind screen supplied with the microphone. Refer also to the instruction manual of the DM-100.

To the MIC terminal you can attach commercially available condenser microphones with their own power supply, and a ∅ 3.5 mm stereo mini plug.

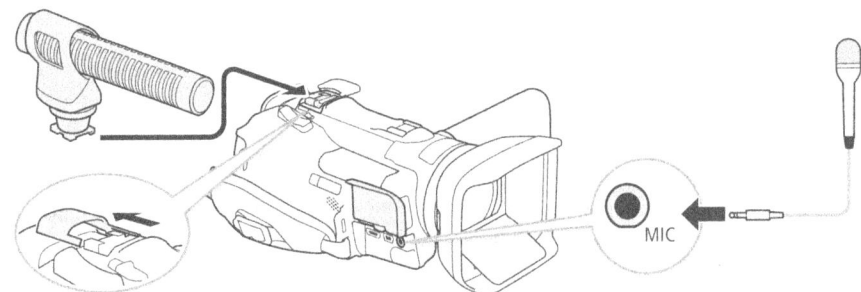

Connect the optional DM-100 Directional Stereo Microphone to the mini advanced shoe (⎙ 71). Connect other external microphones to the MIC terminal.

(i) NOTES

• When using an optional DM-100 Directional Stereo Microphone attached to the camcorder, if you operate the zoom while recording, the microphone may pick up and record lens operation sounds.

• When using an external microphone, if you use the built-in Wi-Fi functions while recording, noise may be recorded due to interference from the wireless communication. With microphones connected to the MIC terminal, if possible, keep the microphone away from the camcorder while recording.

Audio Scenes

You can have the camcorder optimize the audio settings of the built-in microphone by selecting the audio scene that matches your surroundings. This will greatly enhance the sense of "being there".

1 Open the audio scene selection screen.

[FUNC] ❯ [♪⏺ Audio] ❯ [♪STD]*

2 Touch the desired audio scene and then touch [✕].

• If necessary, touch [∧]/[∨] to scroll up/down.

• The icon of the selected audio scene appears at the right of the screen.

* Default option. The button will show the icon of the audio scene currently in use.

Options

[♪STD Standard]: To record most general situations. The camcorder records with standard settings.

[🎤 Music]: To vibrantly record music performances and singing indoors.

[🎪 Festival]: Optimized for recording music outdoors more naturally. Ideal for outdoor events with music.

[🎤 Speech]: Best for recording human voices and dialog.

[🎤 Meeting]: To record people talking while keeping each voice separate, allowing viewers to feel as if they were there.

[🦅 Forest and Birds]:
To record birds and scenes in forests. The camcorder clearly captures sound as it spreads.

[🎬 Noise Suppression]:
To record clips while reducing noise from wind, passing vehicles and similar ambient sound. Ideal for recording at the beach or in places with a lot of noise.

[♪c Custom Setting]:
In [M] mode, this option allows you to adjust the built-in microphone's characteristics (□ 74) according to your needs and preferences.

Settings for each audio scene

	[♪STD Standard]	[🎤 Music]	[🎪 Festival]	[🎤 Speech]	[🎤 Meeting]	[🦅 Forests and Birds]	[🎬 Noise Suppression]	[♪c Custom Setting]
[Mic Level]	[🎤M Manual]: 70	[🎤M Manual]: 70	[🎤M Manual]: 70	[🎤M Manual]: 86	[🎤M Manual]: 94	[🎤M Manual]: 80	[🎤M Manual]: 70	Selected by user (□ 74)
[Built-in Mic Att.]	[OFF Off]	[OFF Off]	[OFF Off]	[OFF Off]	[OFF Off]	[OFF Off]	[OFF Off]	[OFF Off]
[Built-in Mic Wind Screen]	[H Auto (High)]	[L Auto (Low) 🌬/🎤]	[L Auto (Low) 🌬/🎤]	[H Auto (High)]	[H Auto (High)]	[H Auto (High)]	[H Auto (High)]	
[Built-in Mic Freq. Response]	[NORM Normal]	[LHB Boost HF+LF Range]	[NORM Normal]	[MB Boost MF Range]	[MB Boost MF Range]	[LC Low Cut Filter]	[LC Low Cut Filter]	Selected by user (□ 74)
[Built-in Mic Directionality]	[NORM Normal]	[2ch WIDE Wide]	[2ch WIDE Wide]	[2ch MONO Monaural]	[2ch WIDE Wide]	[2ch WIDE Wide]	[2ch MONO Monaural]	
[Audio Limiter]	[ON On]	[ON On]	[ON On]	[ON On]	[ON On]	[ON On]	[ON On]	
[Audio Compressor]	[L Low]	[L Low]	[L Low]	[OFF Off]	[H High]	[L Low]	[OFF Off]	

ⓘ NOTES

- [♪c Custom Setting] is not available in AUTO mode. If the camcorder is set to AUTO mode after having set the audio scene to [♪c Custom Setting], the audio scene will change automatically to [♪STD Standard].

- When using the [🎤 Music] audio scene, to reproduce louder and quieter sounds in music more faithfully, we recommend that you first adjust the audio recording level (□ 74).

- To reproduce the linearity of the music even more faithfully, we recommend that you select the [♪c Custom Setting] audio scene and adjust the audio settings to match those of the [🎤 Music] audio scene, except for setting [Audio Compressor] to [OFF Off] (□ 77).

Adjusting the Audio Recording Level

You can adjust the audio recording levels using the audio screen in the FUNC menu. The audio screen shows the audio input currently selected, whether the audio recording level is adjusted automatically or manually and audio level indicators for CH1/CH2.

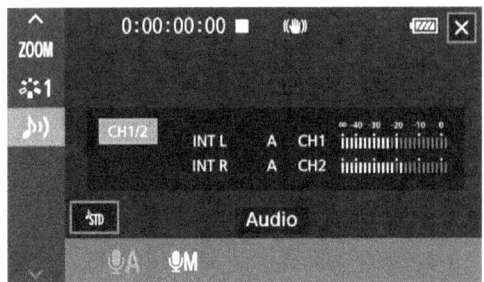

1 Open the audio screen.

   [FUNC] ❯ [♪)) Audio]

2 Touch [♨A Automatic] or [♨M Manual].

   • If you selected automatic adjustment, skip to step 5. If you selected manual adjustment, continue the procedure to adjust the audio recording level.

3 Touch and hold [◀] or [▶] to adjust the recording level as necessary.

   • As a guideline, adjust the audio recording level so that the audio level meter on the screen will go to the right of the −18 dB mark (one mark right of the −20 dB mark) only occasionally.

4 Touch [✖].

(i) NOTES

• When the audio level meter reaches the red point (0 dB), the sound may be distorted.

• If the audio level display is normal but the sound is distorted, activate the microphone's attenuator (□ 74).

• We recommend using headphones to check the sound level while adjusting the audio recording level or when the microphone attenuator is activated.

Advanced Microphone Settings

Microphone Attenuator (Built-in Microphone)

When no external microphone is connected to the MIC terminal, you can activate the built-in microphone's attenuator (20 dB) to prevent audio distortions when the audio level is too high.

Operating modes: [CAMERA] | [M]

1 Select the [♪c Custom Setting] audio scene in advance (□ 72).

2 Select [Built-in Mic Att.].

   MENU ❯ [♪)) 1 Audio Setup] ❯ [Built-in Mic Att.]

3 Touch [**ON** On] and then touch [✖].

   • **ATT** appears at the right of the screen.

Wind Screen (Built-in Microphone)

When no external microphone is connected to the MIC terminal, you can activate the built-in microphone's wind screen. When the wind screen is activated, the camcorder will automatically reduce the sound of wind in the background as necessary when recording outdoors. You can select one of two levels according to the audio recording conditions.

Operating modes: [CAMERA] | [M]

1 Select the [♪c Custom Setting] audio scene in advance (□ 72).
2 Select [Built-in Mic Wind Screen].
   MENU ❯ [♪)) ① Audio Setup] **❯** [Built-in Mic Wind Screen]
3 Touch the desired option and then touch [✕].
   • Depending on the selected setting, 🔽/🎤 or 🔽/🎤 appears at the right of the screen.

Options

[H Auto (High)]:   For a larger wind noise reduction effect. With this setting other low-frequency sounds will be suppressed as well.

[L Auto (Low) 🔽/🎤]:
                     For a smaller wind noise reduction effect. Other low-frequency sounds are mostly unaffected.

[OFF Off]:   The wind screen is turned off.

Frequency Response (Built-in Microphone)

When no external microphone is connected to the MIC terminal, you can apply frequency filters to change the built-in microphone's characteristics according to the audio recording conditions.

Operating modes: [CAMERA] | [M]

1 Select the [♪c Custom Setting] audio scene in advance (□ 72).
2 Select [Built-in Mic Freq. Response].
   MENU ❯ [♪)) ① Audio Setup] **❯** [Built-in Mic Freq. Response]
3 Touch the desired option and then touch [✕].

Options

[NORM Normal]:   Appropriate for balanced sound under most normal recording conditions.
[LB Boost LF Range]:
                     Accentuates the low-frequency range for more powerful sound.
[LC Low Cut Filter]:
                     Filters the low-frequency range to reduce the noise of blowing wind, a car's engine and similar ambient sounds.
[MB Boost MF Range]:
                     Best for recording human voices and dialog.
[LHB Boost HF+LF Range]:
                     Best, for example, for recording live music and to clearly capture the special sound characteristics of a variety of instruments.

Microphone Directionality (Built-in Microphone)

When no external microphone is connected to the MIC terminal, you can change the directionality of the built-in microphone to have more control over how sound is recorded.

Operating modes: CAMERA | M

1 Select the [♪c Custom Setting] audio scene in advance (☐ 72).

2 Select [Built-in Mic Directionality].

MENU ❯ [♪))] ① Audio Setup] ❯ [Built-in Mic Directionality]

3 Touch the desired option and then touch [✕].

Options

[2ch MONO Monaural]: Mono recording that emphasizes sound coming from the front of the camcorder/microphone.

[NORM Normal]: Standard stereo recording; a middle point between the [2ch WIDE Wide] and [2ch MONO Monaural] settings in reach.

[2ch WIDE Wide]: Stereo recording of ambient sound over a more extensive area that adds to the sense of presence of movies.

Audio Limiter

The audio limiter will limit the amplitude of audio signals to prevent audio distortions when sudden, loud sounds are picked up by the camcorder.

Operating modes: CAMERA | AUTO* M

* In AUTO mode only for external microphones.

1 When using the built-in microphone, select the [♪c Custom Setting] audio scene in advance (☐ 72).

• This step is not necessary when using an external microphone.

2 Make sure that [FUNC] ❯ [♪)) Audio] is set to [🎤M Manual] (☐ 74).

3 Select [Audio Limiter].

MENU ❯ [♪))] ① Audio Setup] ❯ [Audio Limiter]

4 Touch [ON On] and then touch [✕].

Audio Compressor

The audio compressor reduces the dynamic range between the loudest and quietest audio levels while maintaining a clear distinction. This can make listening to the audio easier. You can select one of two levels according to the audio recording conditions. The audio compressor can be used only when the audio limiter is activated.

Operating modes: [CAMERA] | [AUTO]* [M]

* In [AUTO] mode only for external microphones.

1 When using the built-in microphone, select the [♪c Custom Setting] audio scene in advance (◻ 72).
 • This step is not necessary when using an external microphone.
2 Select [Audio Compressor].

MENU ❯ [♪))] ① Audio Setup] ❯ [Audio Compressor]

3 Touch the desired option and then touch [✖].

Options

[H High]: Flattens out audio levels more and is best when recording multiple people talking at varying levels, such as during a meeting.

[L Low]: Keeps a clearer distinction between loud and quiet sounds and is best when recording situations such as a musical performance. This setting is effective when the audio level meter goes all the way to the right repeatedly.

[OFF Off]: To record scenes that are not mainly people talking or music performances.

Microphone Attenuator (External Microphones)

In order to prevent audio distortions when the audio level is too high, you can activate the microphone attenuator (20 dB) for an external microphone connected to the MIC terminal or for the optional DM-100 Directional Stereo Microphone attached to the camcorder's mini advanced shoe.

Operating modes: [CAMERA] | [AUTO] [M]

1 Select the [♪c Custom Setting] audio scene in advance (◻ 72).
2 Select [MIC Att.] or [„♪" Mic Att.].

MENU ❯ [♪))] ② Audio Setup] ❯ [MIC Att.] (MIC terminal) or [„♪" Mic Att.] (DM-100)

3 Touch [ON On] and then touch [✖].
 • appears at the right of the screen.

Low-Cut Filter (MIC Terminal)

You can activate the low-cut filter for an external microphone connected to the MIC terminal. This can help, for example, to reduce the sound of wind in the background when recording outdoors. When recording in surroundings unaffected by wind or if you want to record low-frequency sounds, we recommend turning off the low-cut filter.

Operating modes: [CAMERA] | [AUTO] [M]

1 Select [MIC Low Cut].

MENU ❯ [♪))] ② Audio Setup] ❯ [MIC Low Cut]

2 Touch [ON On] and then touch [✖].

Using Headphones

Connect headphones with a Ø 3.5 mm stereo mini plug to the ∩ (headphone) terminal for playback or to monitor the recorded audio.

Operating modes: [CAMERA] [MEDIA] | [AUTO] [M]

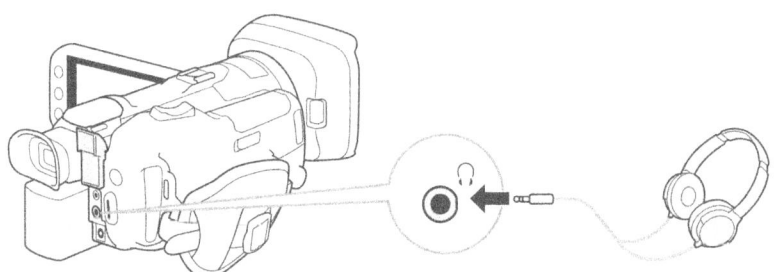

1 Select [Headphone Volume].

   MENU ❯ [♪))] 2 * Audio Setup] ❯ [Headphone Volume]
   * Page 1 in [MEDIA] mode.

2 Touch [∩)] or [∩))] to adjust the volume and then touch [✖].

   • You can also drag your finger along the volume bar.

To adjust the volume during playback
During playback, you can also adjust the headphones volume in the same way you adjust the speaker's volume (□ 92).

ⓘ IMPORTANT

• When using headphones, make sure to lower the volume to an appropriate level.

Color Bars/Audio Reference Signal

You can have the camcorder generate color bars and a 1 kHz audio reference signal to calibrate an external monitor. The color bars and audio reference signal can be output from the HDMI OUT terminal and ⌒ (headphone) terminal*.

* Audio reference signal only.

Operating modes: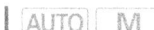

Recording Color Bars

You can choose between SMPTE and ARIB color bars.

1 Select [Color Bars].

MENU ❯ [🗂 ③ Recording Setup] ❯ [Color Bars]

2 Touch the desired option and then touch [✕].

- The selected color bars appear on the screen and will be recorded when you press the REC button.

ⓘ NOTES

- You cannot change the type of color bars while recording or when pre-recording is activated.

Recording an Audio Reference Signal

The camcorder can output a 1 kHz audio reference signal with the color bars.

1 Select [1 kHz Tone].

MENU ❯ [🗂 ③ Recording Setup] ❯ [1 kHz Tone]

2 Touch the desired option and then touch [✕].

- You can select one of three audio levels (–12 dB, –18 dB, –20 dB) or select [**OFF** Off] to turn off the signal.
- The signal is output at the selected level and will be recorded when you press the REC button.

Pre-Recording

When pre-recording is activated, the camcorder starts recording continuously into a temporary memory (approx. 3 seconds) so when you press the REC button, the clip will contain also a few seconds of video and audio recorded before you pressed the button.

Operating modes: CAMERA | AUTO M

1 Press the PRE REC button.
- Pre-recording is activated and 🕒 appears at the top of the screen.
- Press the button again to turn off pre-recording.

2 Press the REC button.
- The clip recorded on the card will include a few seconds of video and audio recorded before the REC button was pressed.

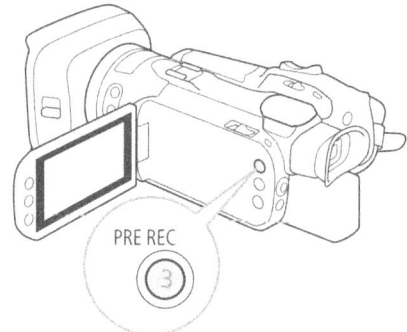

(i) NOTES

- The camcorder will not record the full 3 seconds prior to pressing the REC button if the button was pressed within 3 seconds of having turned on pre-recording or having finished the previous recording.
- Pre-recording will be deactivated in the following cases:
  - If the position of the mode switch was changed.
  - If the menu was opened.
  - If the shooting mode, white balance or look was changed.
- About the time code when pre-recording is activated:
  - The time code of the clip will start a few seconds before the REC button was pressed.
  - The time code will be recorded with the running mode set to [FREERUN Free Run].
  - If the time code mode was set to [REGEN. Regen.], or to [PRESET Preset] with [RECRUN Rec Run] running mode, the time code running mode will be changed automatically to [FREERUN Free Run] when pre-recording is activated.
  - When pre-recording is turned off, the time code running mode will return to its previous setting.

Using the Optional RC-V100 Remote Controller

You can connect the optional RC-V100 Remote Controller to the camcorder's REMOTE terminal in order to control the camcorder (including advanced recording functions) from a distance. The remote controller lets you turn the camcorder on, navigate the menus and remotely control the aperture and shutter speed, and more. Use the cable supplied with the remote controller to connect it to the camcorder. For details on how to connect and use the remote controller, refer to its instruction manual.

Operating modes: CAMERA MEDIA | AUTO M

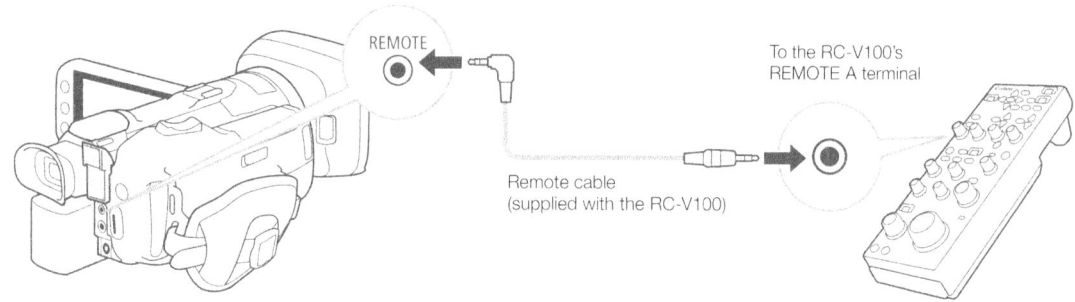

1 Turn off the camcorder and connect the optional RC-V100 Remote Controller to the camcorder.
2 Turn on the camcorder and select [REMOTE Terminal].
   MENU ❯ [♀ 2 System Setup] ❯ [REMOTE Terminal]
3 Touch [RC-V100 RC-V100 (REMOTE A)] and then touch [✕].

Options

[RC-V100 RC-V100 (REMOTE A)]:
   Select this option to use the optional RC-V100 Remote Controller.
[Std. Standard]:   Select this option to use commercially available remote controls.

(i) NOTES

- The following controls on the remote controller will not operate the camcorder:
  - CUSTOM PICT. button
  - AGC button
  - AUTO KNEE button
  - KNEE POINT, KNEE SLOPE dials
  - BLACK GAMMA LEVEL dial
  - SHARPNESS LEVEL dial
  - WHITE BALANCE R and B dials
  - MASTER BLACK R and B dials
  - MASTER PEDESTAL dial
  - AUTO IRIS button
  - CANCEL button

Using the Optional GP-E2 GPS Receiver

When the optional GP-E2 GPS Receiver is connected to the camcorder's USB terminal, the camcorder will automatically record the GPS information (longitude, latitude and altitude) and coordinated universal time (UTC) with the clips and photos you record.

For details about attaching and configuring the receiver, refer to the instruction manual of the GP-E2.

Operating modes: CAMERA | AUTO M

Connecting the GPS Receiver

Turn off the camcorder and the receiver. Connect the receiver to the camcorder's USB terminal using the USB cable*. While recording, place the receiver in the carrying case* and attach it to the camcorder's grip belt or carry it on your person.

* Supplied with the receiver.

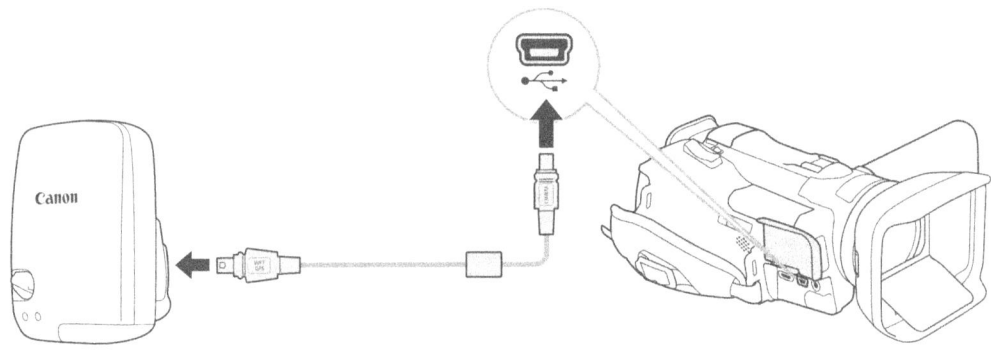

To adjust the date and time automatically according to the GPS data

You can set [♀ System Setup] ❯ [GPS Auto Time Setting] to [ON Auto Update], to have the camcorder automatically adjust its date and time settings according to the information received from the GPS signal. The date and time will be updated automatically the first time a correct GPS signal is acquired after turning on the camcorder.

- While the automatic date/time adjustment is activated, the [♀ System Setup] ❯ [Date/Time] setting will not be available.
- The time will not be updated while recording or when Browser Remote is activated (◻ 111).

ⓘ IMPORTANT

- In certain countries and regions, the use of GPS may be restricted. Therefore, be sure to use GPS in accordance with the laws and regulations of your country or region. Be particularly careful when traveling outside your home country.
- Be careful about using GPS functions where the operation of electronic devices is restricted.
- The GPS information recorded with clips and photos may contain data that can lead others to locate or identify you. Be careful when sharing geotagged recordings with others or when uploading them to the Web.
- Do not leave the GPS receiver near strong electromagnetic fields such as near powerful magnets and motors.

(i) NOTES

• The camcorder is not compatible with the receiver's digital compass and positioning interval functions. Also, the [Set Now] option is not available for the [GPS Auto Time Setting] setting.

• Initial GPS signal reception will take longer after replacing the power source or when first turning on the camcorder after a period of having been turned off.

• The GPS information recorded with clips corresponds to the location at the start of the recording.

• Do not lay cables connected to the HDMI OUT terminal near the receiver. Doing so may negatively affect the GPS signal.

83

4

CUSTOM Dial and Button

You can assign to the CUSTOM button and dial one of several frequently used functions. You can then adjust the selected function using the CUSTOM button and dial, without having to access the menu.

Operating modes: | M

1 Select [CUSTOM Dial & Button].

   MENU ❯ [❤ ③ System Setup] ❯ [CUSTOM Dial & Button]

2 Touch the desired option and then touch [✗].

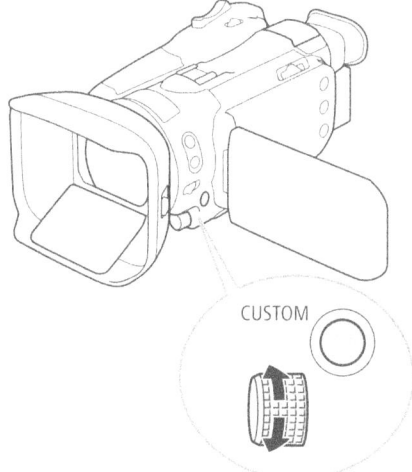

Options

[TV/AV/M Tv/Av/M]:   When the shooting mode is set to **Tv** or **Av**, turn the CUSTOM dial to adjust the shutter speed or aperture value, respectively.
When the shooting mode is set to **M**, press the CUSTOM button repeatedly to select the value you wish to adjust (aperture value → shutter speed → gain value). While the desired value is highlighted in orange, turn the dial to adjust it.

[GAIN AGC Limit]: Press the CUSTOM button to turn the AGC limit on/off. When the AGC limit is activated, turn the dial to set the maximum gain value.

[Ⓩ Exposure Comp.]:
Press the CUSTOM button to lock the exposure and, if necessary, turn the dial to compensate the exposure (exposure lock + compensation).

[OFF Off]:   Disables the CUSTOM button and dial.

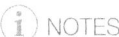 NOTES

• Instead of the procedure above, you can press and hold the CUSTOM button to display a quick menu of the options. Use the CUSTOM dial to select the desired option and then press the CUSTOM button.

Assignable Buttons

The camcorder offers 5 assignable buttons on the camcorder's body and an onscreen button (touch operation) to which you can assign various functions (assignable buttons). Assign often-used functions to the buttons you find most convenient, to personalize the camcorder to your needs and preferences.

The names of the buttons printed on the camcorder also indicate their default settings. The onscreen assignable button will show only the icon of the function currently assigned to it.

Operating modes: CAMERA | AUTO M

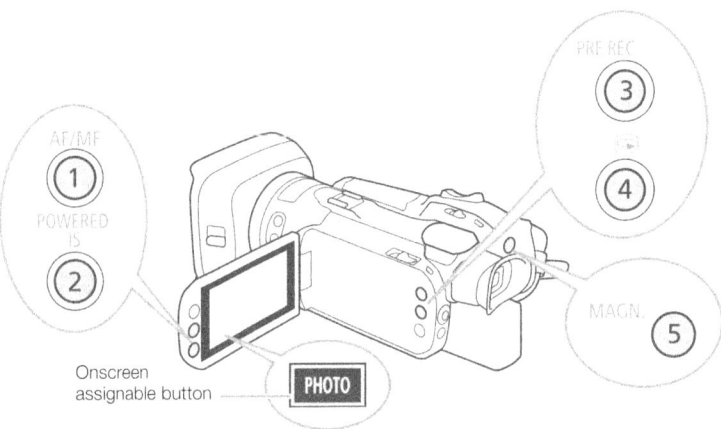

Onscreen
assignable button

PHOTO

Changing the Assigned Function

1 Physical buttons: Press the MENU button and, while holding it pressed down, press the assignable button whose function you wish to change.
Onscreen assignable button: Open the function selection screen with the menu setting.

MENU ❯ [Y 3 System Setup] ❯ [Onscreen Assignable Button]

• A list of available functions appears with the current function assigned to the button highlighted.

• You can use the menu also for physical assignable buttons. The corresponding settings ([Assignable Button 1] to [Assignable Button 5]) can be found under pages 2 and 3 in the [Y System Setup] menu.

2 Touch the desired function and then touch [✕].

• If necessary, touch [▲]/[▼] to scroll up/down.

3 Press the assignable button (or touch the onscreen assignable button) to use the assigned function as described in the following table.

86

Assignable functions

Function name	Description	📖
[BLC Always On]	Turns the constant backlight correction function on/off.	62
[Face Only AF]	Switches between standard autofocus and autofocus only when a face is detected.	51
[Focus Guide]	Turns the Dual Pixel Focus Guide function on/off.	46
[WB WB Priority]	Switches between the current white balance setting and a priority white balance setting registered with the ['🎥 Camera Setup] ❯ [Set WB Priority] setting.	123
[AF/MF AF/MF]	Switches between autofocus and manual focus.	45
[Powered IS]	Turns powered IS on/off.	56
[Pre REC]	Turns pre-recording on/off.	80
[REC REVIEW Rec Review]	Reviews the last clip recorded.	37
[MAGN. Magnification]	Turns magnification on/off.	48
[PHOTO Photo]	Records a photo.	36
[OFF Off]	No function assigned – the button is disabled.	—

Saving and Loading Camcorder Settings

After you adjust settings in the various menus, you can save those settings on an SD card. You can load those settings at a later date or on another GX10 camcorder so that you can use that camcorder in the exact same way.

88

Camcorder settings can only be saved on or loaded from the SD card in card slot B.

Operating modes: [CAMERA] | [AUTO] [M]

Saving Camcorder Settings

1 Insert the SD card where you want to save the camcorder's settings into SD card slot B.

2 Select [Save].

MENU ❯ [❥ 4 System Setup] ❯ [Backup Menu Settings B] ❯ [Save]

3 Touch [Yes].

- The camcorder's menu settings will be saved to the card. If menu settings were previously saved, the old file will be overwritten by the current menu settings.

4 When the confirmation message appears, touch [OK].

Loading Camcorder Settings

1 Insert an SD card that contains previously saved camcorder settings into SD card slot B.

2 Select [Load].

MENU ❯ [❥ 4 System Setup] ❯ [Backup Menu Settings B] ❯ [Load]

3 Touch [Yes].

- The camcorder's menu settings will be replaced by the settings saved on the card. Then, the screen will turn black momentarily and the camcorder will restart.

(i) NOTES

- Camcorder settings files are exclusively compatible for use only with GX10 camcorders.
- Passwords/encryption keys that were set by the user under [❥ System Setup] ❯ [Network Settings] are not saved with this operation. After loading previously saved menu settings, set up the necessary network passwords again.

Basic Playback

This section explains how to play back clips and photos. For details on playing back recordings using an external monitor, refer to *Connecting to an External Monitor or Recorder* (◻ 99).

Operating modes: MEDIA |

The Playback Index Screen

1 Set the power switch to MEDIA.

- The camcorder switches to MEDIA mode and the clip index screen appears.

2 Look for the clip you wish to play back.

- Swipe left/right or touch [◀]/[▶] to check other index pages.
- To view photos or play back recordings on the other SD card, change the index screen.

3 Touch the thumbnail of the desired clip to start playback (◻ 90).

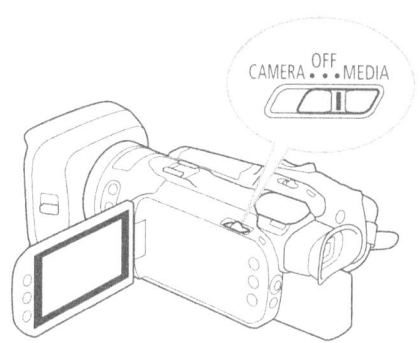

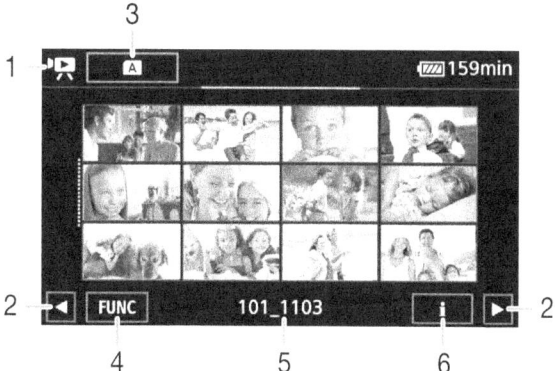

1 🎥: Clip index screen
   📷: Photo index screen.
2 Display the next/previous index page.
   You can also swipe left/right on the screen.
3 Index screen button: Touch to change the index screen.

4 [FUNC] button: Clip/photo operations (◻ 93).
5 Folder name. The last 4 digits indicate the recording date (1103 = November 3).
6 Clips only: Clip information (◻ 92).

Changing the Index Screen

You can change the index screen to switch between playing back clips (🎥) and photos (📷) or to play back recordings from a different SD card (Ⓐ/Ⓑ).

Touch the index screen button and then touch the desired index screen.

• You can also press the 【ᖫ】button on the supplied wireless controller to open the index selection screen.

Options

[Ⓐ 🎥 Movies]: Clips recorded on SD card A.

[Ⓑ 🎥 Movies]: Clips recorded on SD card B.

[Ⓐ 📷 Photos]: Photos recorded on SD card A.

[Ⓑ 📷 Photos]: Photos recorded on SD card B.

Playing Back Recordings

1 In the index screen, touch the thumbnail of the desired recording.

• **Clips**: Playback will start from the selected clip until the last clip in the index screen.
Photos: The selected photo will be displayed. Swipe left/right to view other photos.

2 Touch the screen to display the playback controls.

• During video playback, the playback controls will disappear automatically after a few seconds. In video playback pause or for photos, touch the screen again to hide the playback controls.

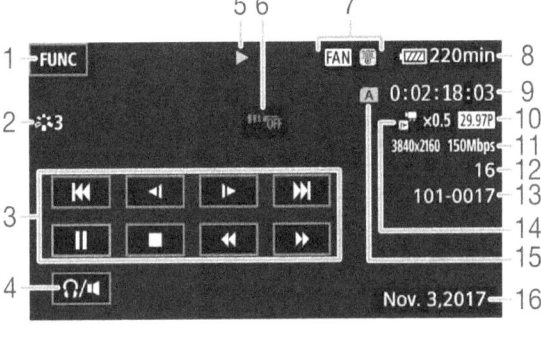
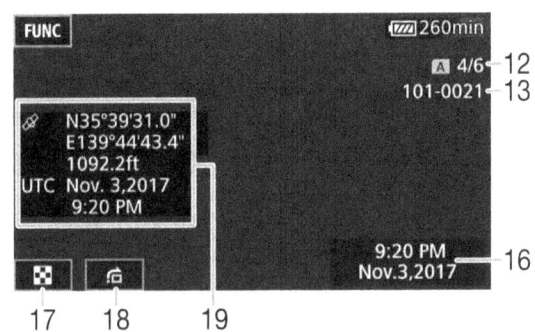

1 [FUNC] button: Clip/photo operations (□ 93)	11 Resolution and bit rate (□ 42)
2 Look (□ 67)	12 Clips: Clip number
3 Clip playback controls (□ 91)	Photos: Photo number / Total number of photos
4 Volume (□ 92)	13 File number (□ 125)
5 Clip playback operation (□ 91)	14 Slow & fast motion rate (□ 44)
6 Wireless controller disabled (□ 127)	15 SD card selected for playback (□ 90)
7 Fan operation and temperature warning (□ 134)	16 Data code (□ 124)
8 Remaining battery charge (□ 39)	17 Return the photo index screen
9 Time code (□ 68)	18 Photo jump (□ 91)
10 Frame rate (□ 42)	19 GPS information* (□ 82)

* Only when the optional GP-E2 GPS receiver was used when recording the photo.

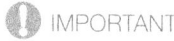 IMPORTANT

- Observe the following precautions while the ACCESS indicator is illuminated in red. Failing to do so may result in permanent data loss.
  - Do not open the SD card compartment cover.
  - Do not disconnect the power source or turn off the camcorder.
  - Do not change the camcorder's operating mode.
- You may not be able to play back with this camcorder movies recorded on an SD card using another device.

(i) NOTES

- Depending on the recording conditions, you may notice brief stops in video or sound playback between clips.
- The following image files may not be displayed correctly.
  - Images not recorded with this camcorder.
  - Images edited on a computer.
  - Images whose file names have been changed.

Playback Controls

The following playback types are available using the onscreen controls. Using the joystick, push the joystick to select the desired button and then press the joystick. For clip playback, you can also use the playback buttons on the supplied wireless controller.

Clip playback controls

Playback type	Operation	Onscreen icon
Fast playback*	During playback, touch [◄◄] / [►►]. • Touch repeatedly to increase the playback speed to approximately 5x → 15x → 60x the normal speed. • During fast playback, touch [►] to return to playback at normal speed.	x00►► ◄◄x00
Slow playback*	Touch [◄I] / [I►]. • Touch repeatedly to change the playback speed to approximately 1/4 → 1/8 the normal speed.	x1/0I► ◄Ix1/0
Frame reverse/advance*	During playback pause, touch [◄II] / [II►].	◄II II►
Skip to the beginning of the current clip	Touch [I◄◄].	—
Skip to the beginning of the previous clip	Touch [I◄◄] twice.	—
Skip to the beginning of the next clip	Touch [►►I].	—
Pause/resume playback	During playback, touch [II] to pause. During playback pause, touch to [►] to resume normal playback.	II ►
Stop playback	Touch [■] to stop playback and return to the index screen.	—

* There is no audio during this playback mode.

Photo playback controls

Playback type	Operation
Return to the photo index screen	Touch [▦].
Photo jump	Touch [⌂] to display the scroll bar. Touch [◄] / [►], or drag your finger along the scroll bar, to find the desired photo. Touch [↩] to return to single photo view.

(i) NOTES

- During fast/slow playback, you may notice some anomalies (blocky video artifacts, banding, etc.) in the playback picture.
- The speed indicated on the screen is approximate.
- Slow reverse playback will look the same as continuous frame reverse.

Adjusting the volume

During playback, audio will be output from the monaural built-in speaker. You can connect a pair of headphones to the ∩ (headphone) terminal to listen to the audio in stereo.

1 During playback, touch the screen to display the playback controls.

2 Touch [∩/◀].

3 Touch [◀)]/[∩)] or [◀))]/[∩))] to adjust the volume and then touch [↰].

- You can also drag your finger along the respective volume bar.

Displaying Clip Information

1 In the clip index screen touch [i] and then touch the desired clip.

- The [Clip Info] screen will be displayed.
- Touch [◀] / [▶] to view the information for the previous/next clip.

2 Touch [↰] twice to return to the index screen.

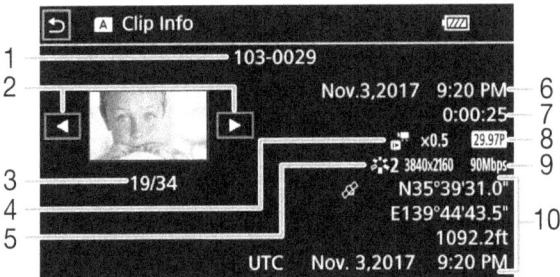

1	File number (□ 125)	7	Clip duration
2	Display the information for the previous/next clip	8	Frame rate (□ 42)
3	Clip number / Total number of clips	9	Resolution and bit rate (□ 42)
4	Slow & fast motion rate (□ 44)	10	GPS information* (□ 82)
5	Look (□ 67)		(location at the start of recording)
6	Date and time at the start of recording		

* Only when the optional GP-E2 GPS receiver was used when recording the clip.

Clip and Photo Operations

Operating modes: MEDIA |

Deleting Clips and Photos

You can delete clips and photos you are not interested in keeping.

Deleting Clips and Photos from the Index Screen

1 Open the desired index screen (📖 89).
- To delete all the clips or photos recorded on the same date (saved in the same folder), drag your finger left/right until a clip or photo you want to delete appears.

2 Select [Delete].

[FUNC] ❯ [Delete]

3 Touch the desired option and then touch [Yes].
- When you touch [Select], perform the following procedure to select the individual recordings you want to delete before touching [Yes].
- Touch [Stop] to interrupt the operation while it is in progress. Some recordings may be deleted nevertheless.

4 When the confirmation message appears, touch [OK].

To select individual recordings

1 Touch the individual clips/photos you want to delete.
- A checkmark ✓ will appear on the recordings you touch. The total number of selected clips/photos will appear next to the ☑ icon.
- Touch a selected clip or photo to remove the checkmark. To remove all checkmarks at once, touch [Remove All] ❯ [Yes].

2 After selecting all the desired recordings, touch [OK].

Options

<folder name>:   Deletes all the clips or photos recorded on a particular date. The last 4 digits of the folder name in the button indicate the recording date (1103 = November 3).

[Select]:   You can select the individual clips or photos you want to delete.

[All Clips], [All Photos]:
            Deletes all the clips or photos.

Deleting a Single Clip

1 Play back the desired clip (📖 90).
2 Touch the screen to display the playback controls and then delete the clip.

[❚❚] ❯ [FUNC] ❯ [Delete] ❯ [Yes]

3 When the confirmation message appears, touch [OK].

Deleting a Single Photo

1 Play back the desired photo (📖 90).
2 Touch the screen to display the playback controls and then delete the photo.

[FUNC] ❯ [Delete] ❯ [🗑 Proceed] ❯ [Yes]

3 Drag your finger left/right to select another photo to delete or touch [✖].

IMPORTANT

- **Be careful when deleting recordings. Once deleted, they cannot be recovered.**
- Save copies of important recordings before deleting them (🕮 101).
- Observe the following precautions while the ACCESS indicator is illuminated in red (while recordings are being deleted).
  - Do not open the SD card compartment cover.
  - Do not disconnect the power source or turn off the camcorder.
  - Do not change the camcorder's operating mode.

NOTES

- Photos that were protected with other devices cannot be deleted with this camcorder.
- To delete all recordings and make all recordable space available again you may prefer to initialize the SD card (🕮 31).

Trimming Clips

You can trim clips by removing everything up to a certain point or everything after a certain point.

1 Play back the desired clip (🕮 90).

2 Touch the screen to display the playback controls and then open the trimming screen.

[❚❚] ❯ [FUNC] ❯ [Trim]

3 Bring the clip to a precise point, if necessary.

- The point at which the clip will be trimmed is indicated by the ⊤ marker.
- Playback controls will appear on the screen (🕮 91). Use any special playback modes as necessary to locate the desired point.

4 Select the desired trimming options and trim the clip.

[Trim] ❯ [Trim Before Marker] or [Trim After Marker] ❯ [Save as New] or [Overwrite]

- With the first set of options you can select, respectively, to trim before or after the ⊤ mark.
  With the second set of options you can select, respectively, to save the trimmed clip as a new clip or to overwrite the existing clip.
- If you selected [Save as New], you can touch [Stop] and then [OK] to interrupt the operation while it is in progress.

NOTES

- In the index screen, clips trimmed with the [Trim Before Marker] option appear with a special playback icon instead of the usual thumbnail.
- In the trimming screen, the frame reverse/advance button will jump in 1-frame intervals. The positions where trimming is possible are 1 GOP (0.5 second) apart.
- The clip is trimmed at the start/end of the GOP that includes the frame indicated with the marker.

Copying Clips and Photos

You can copy clips and photos from one SD card to the other.

1 Open the desired index screen (□ 89).

- To copy all the clips or photos recorded on the same date (saved in the same folder), drag your finger left/right until a clip or photo you want to copy appears.

2 Select [Copy ([A] ◆ [B])] or [Copy ([B] ◆ [A])].

[FUNC] ❯ [Copy ([A] ◆ [B])] or [Copy ([B] ◆ [A])]

3 Touch the desired option and then touch [Yes].

- When you select [Select], perform the following procedure to select the individual recordings you want to copy before touching [Yes].
- Touch [Stop] to interrupt the operation while it is in progress.

4 When the confirmation message appears, touch [OK].

To select individual recordings

1 Touch on the individual clips/photos you want to copy.

- A checkmark ✓ will appear on the recordings you touch. The total number of selected clips/photos will appear next to the ✔ icon.
- Touch a selected clip or photo to remove the checkmark. To remove all checkmarks at once, touch [Remove All] ❯ [Yes].

2 After selecting all the desired recordings, touch [OK].

Options

<folder name>: Copies all the clips or photos recorded on a particular date. The last 4 digits of the folder name in the button indicate the recording date (1103 = November 3).

[Select]: You can select the individual clips or photos you want to copy.

[All Clips], [All Photos]:
Copies all the clips or photos.

🛈 IMPORTANT

- Observe the following precautions while the ACCESS indicator is illuminated in red. Failing to do so may result in permanent data loss.
  - Do not open the SD card compartment cover.
  - Do not disconnect the power source or turn off the camcorder.
  - Do not change the camcorder's operating mode.

ⓘ NOTES

- In the following cases, you will not be able to copy recordings to SD card B:
  - If the SD card compartment cover is open.
  - If the LOCK switch on the destination SD card is set to prevent writing.
  - If a file number (□ 125) cannot be created because the number of folders and files in the card has reached its maximum.
- If there is not enough space on the destination SD card, as many photos as possible will be copied before stopping the operation.
- Video stream files over 4 GB in size cannot be copied onto SDHC cards.

Recovering Clips

Some actions, such as suddenly turning off the camcorder or removing the SD card while data is being recorded, can cause data errors in the recorded clip. You may be able to recover clips with corrupted data with the following procedure.

1 Open the index screen with the clip you wish to recover (☐ 89).

2 Touch the corrupted clip (a clip with the ? icon instead of a thumbnail image).

3 When [Attempt to recover the data?] is displayed, touch [Yes].

    • The camcorder will attempt to recover the corrupted data.

4 When the confirmation message appears, touch [OK].

ⓘ NOTES

• In the index screen, recovered clips appear with a special playback icon instead of the usual thumbnail.
• This procedure may delete clips shorter than 0.5 seconds in length.
• In some cases, it may not be possible to recover the data. This is more likely when the file system is corrupted or the SD card is physically damaged.
• Only clips recorded with this camcorder can be recovered. Photos cannot be recovered.

Video Output Configuration

The video signal output from the HDMI™ OUT terminal depends on the clip's video configuration and on various menu settings. The video signal output from the HDMI OUT terminal can also change depending on the capabilities of the connected monitor.

Operating modes: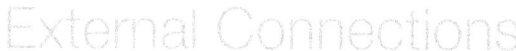

Video Output Configuration (Internal Recording Priority)

Refer to the following table for the video output configuration from the HDMI OUT terminal, depending on the video configuration used for recordings on an SD card (□ 42) or the video configuration of the clip being played back. The video signal can also change depending on the capabilities of the connected monitor.

Video configuration of the clip		HDMI maximum resolution[1]	HDMI OUT terminal video signal
Resolution	Frame rate		
3840x2160	59.94P 29.97P 23.98P	[3840x2160]	3840x2160 YCbCr 4:2:2 8 bit[2]
		[1920x1080]	1920x1080 YCbCr 4:2:2 8 bit
1920x1080	59.94P 29.97P 23.98P	—	1920x1080 YCbCr 4:2:2 8 bit, 720x480 YCbCr 4:2:2 8 bit[3]
1280x720	59.94P 29.97P	[1920x1080]	1920x1080, 720x480 YCbCr 4:2:2 8 bit[3]
		[1280x720]	1280x720, 720x480 YCbCr 4:2:2 8 bit[3]

[1] [🖵 Display Setup] ❯ [HDMI Max Resolution] setting.
[2] YCbCr 4:2:0 8 bit when the frame rate is set to 59.94P.
[3] Only when the frame rate is set to 59.94P.

Video Output Configuration (External Recording Only)

Refer to the following table for the video output configuration from the HDMI OUT terminal when the camcorder is set to external recording-only mode (□ 99).

Internal/external recording[1]	Video configuration for external recording[2]	HDMI OUT terminal video signal
[HDMI External Rec Only (HDMI)]	[3840x2160 59.94P YCC420 8bit]	3840x2160 YCbCr 4:2:0 8 bit
	[3840x2160 29.97P YCC422 8bit]	3840x2160 YCbCr 4:2:2 8 bit
	[1920x1080 59.94P YCC422 10bit]	1920x1080 YCbCr 4:2:2 10 bit
	[1920x1080 29.97P YCC422 10bit]	1920x1080 YCbCr 4:2:2 10 bit

[1] [Recording Setup] ❯ [Internal/External Rec] setting.
[2] [Recording Setup] ❯ [External Rec Video Config.] setting.

Connecting to an External Monitor or Recorder

Operating modes: CAMERA MEDIA | AUTO M

Connection Diagram

We recommend that you power the camcorder from a power outlet using the AC adapter.

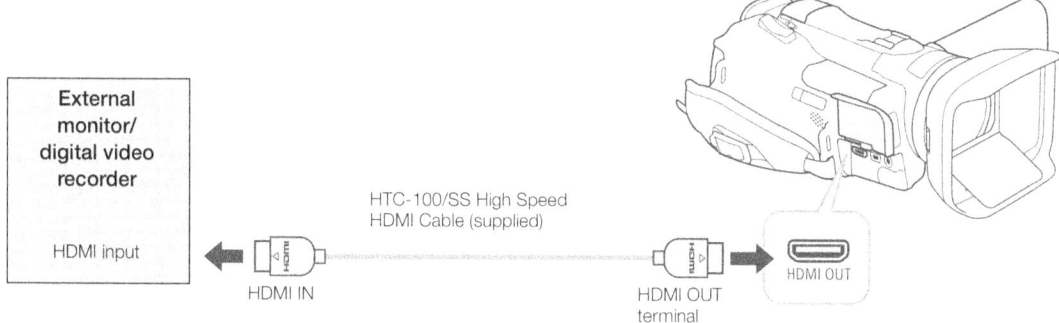

External monitor/digital video recorder

HDMI input

HDMI IN

HTC-100/SS High Speed HDMI Cable (supplied)

HDMI OUT terminal

HDMI OUT

Recording Video Using an External Recorder

In order to record video and audio on an external recorder connected to the camcorder's HDMI OUT terminal, you must set the camcorder in external recording-only mode. Refer also to the external recorder's instruction manual for details on how to record.

Operating modes: CAMERA | AUTO M

1 Select [Internal/External Rec].

MENU ❯ [📷 ① Recording Setup] ❯ [Internal/External Rec]

2 Touch [HDMI External Rec Only (HDMI)] and then touch [�].

3 Select the configuration of the output signal.

[External Rec Video Config.] ❯ Desired option ❯ [✕]

• For details, refer to the *Video Output Configuration* table (□ 97).

ⓘ NOTES

• Depending on the external recorder used, you may not be able to record on the external recorder using the selected output video configuration.

• After connecting the camcorder to an external recorder, make test recordings using the video configuration(s) you plan to use and check the recordings made by the external recorder.

• You can set [📷 Recording Setup] ❯ [Rec Command] to [ON On] to use the camcorder's REC button to control also the recording operation of external recorders compatible with recording commands. While [Rec Command] is set to [ON On], the [♀ System Setup] ❯ [Auto Power Off] setting (power saving mode) will be disabled.

• About the time code during external recording-only mode:
  - The time code mode is automatically set to [PRESET Preset].
  - When the camcorder is set back to internal recording-priority mode, the time code mode will return to its previous setting.

Connecting an External Monitor

The HDMI OUT terminal offers a digital connection and outputs both the video and audio signals. You can output also the time code signal and onscreen displays (□ 126). The audio output signal will be 2-channel linear PCM audio (16-bit, 48 kHz sampling).

Operating modes: CAMERA MEDIA | AUTO M

1 Select [Output Terminal].

MENU ❯ [📷 1 Display Setup] ❯ [Output Terminal]

2 Touch [HDMI HDMI] to activate the HDMI OUT terminal and then touch [✕].

3 Select [HDMI Max Resolution].

MENU ❯ [📷 1 Display Setup] ❯ [HDMI Max Resolution]

4 Touch the desired maximum resolution and then touch [✕].

  • For details, refer to the *Video Output Configuration* table (□ 97).

5 CAMERA mode only: If necessary, output also the time code signal.

MENU ❯ [📷 2 Recording Setup] ❯ [HDMI Time Code] ❯ [ON On] ❯ [✕]

ⓘ NOTES

• When slow & fast motion recording is activated, the time code signal cannot be output from the HDMI OUT terminal.

• The HDMI OUT terminal is for output only. Do not connect the camcorder to another device's output terminal using the HDMI OUT terminal as this will cause a malfunction.

• Correct operation cannot be guaranteed when connecting the camcorder to DVI monitors.

• Video may not be output correctly depending on the monitor.

• You can set both [📷 Recording Setup] ❯ [Rec Command] and [HDMI Time Code] to [ON On] to use the camcorder's REC button to control also the recording operation of an external recorder connected to the HDMI OUT terminal. The camcorder's time code signal will be output as well.

• The time code signal will not be output from the HDMI OUT terminal in the following cases.
  - In MEDIA mode.
  - During SD (720x480) output.
  - When slow & fast motion recording is activated.

• When the resolution is set to [3840x2160 (150 Mbps)] and the frame rate is set to 59.94P (□ 42), to view the camcorder's output signal on a TV or external monitor connected using the supplied High Speed HDMI cable, the TV or external monitor must be compatible with 4K/60p video.

Working with Clips on a Computer

You can use the software Data Import Utility to save your clips. Refer to PIXELA's website below to download the software and check the latest information. For other inquires regarding the software, consult a Canon Service Center.

http://www.pixela.co.jp/oem/canon/e/index_c.html

Saving Clips Using Data Import Utility

- Save clips to the computer using a card reader.
- Join relay clips (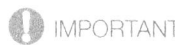 43) that were saved on separate SD cards, and save them as a single clip.
- Join clips split at the 4 GB maximum file size, and save them as a single clip.

For more details, including system requirements and how to install the software, check the Data Import Utility Software Guide, a PDF file in the [\Manual] folder of the downloaded compressed file that contains the software.

IMPORTANT

- Before using Data Import Utility to save clips on the computer, do not access or manipulate the files on the SD card with other software. Failing to do so may result in not being able to save the files with Data Import Utility.

7

About the Network Functions

You can connect the camcorder to a Wi-Fi network to use the following network functions.

Network functions and connection types

Network function	Description	Wi-Fi Infrastructure[1]	Wi-Fi Camera Access Point[2]	📖
Browser Remote	Control the camcorder remotely from the Web browser of a connected device.	–	●	111
FTP File Transfer	Transfer clips recorded with the camcorder to another device connected to the network using the FTP protocol.	●	–	119

[1] Connection to a Wi-Fi network via an external access point (wireless router, etc.)
[2] Direct connection to one Wi-Fi-enabled device where the camcorder itself serves as the Wi-Fi access point.

Before using the network functions

- The instructions in this chapter assume you already have a correctly configured and working network, network device(s) and/or Wi-Fi access point. If necessary, refer to the documentation provided with the network devices you plan to use.
- Configuring the network settings requires adequate knowledge about configuring and using wireless (Wi-Fi) networks. Canon cannot provide support regarding network configurations.

IMPORTANT

- Data transmitted over networks is not encrypted.
- Canon shall not be liable for any loss of data or damage resulting from incorrect network configuration or settings. Additionally, Canon shall not be liable for any loss or damage caused by the use of network functions.
- Using an unprotected Wi-Fi network can expose your data to monitoring by unauthorized third parties. Be aware of the risks involved.

(i) NOTES

- **About the Wi-Fi antenna**: When using the camcorder's Wi-Fi functions, do not cover the Wi-Fi antenna with your hand or other object. Covering it may interfere with wireless signals.
- Do not lay cables connected to the HDMI OUT terminal near the Wi-Fi antenna. Doing so may negatively affect the wireless communication over Wi-Fi.
- Do not open the SD card compartment cover while using network functions.

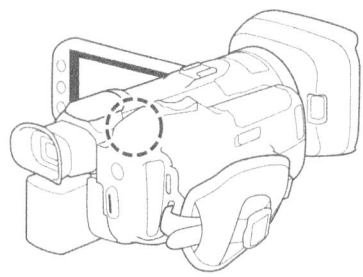

Wi-Fi antenna

Connecting to a Wi-Fi Network

The camcorder is Wi-Fi certified and can connect to access points (wireless router, etc.) and network devices compliant with the 802.11a/b/g/n protocol and that are Wi-Fi certified (bear the logo shown on the right). The Wi-Fi connection's functionality and applicable restrictions may vary depending on the Wi-Fi network used. Note that using an unprotected Wi-Fi connection can expose your data to monitoring by unauthorized third parties. Be aware of the risks involved.

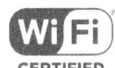

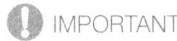

You can connect the camcorder to a Wi-Fi network in Infrastructure mode (using an access point), or directly to one network device in Camera Access Point mode. The type of connection you can use depends on the network function you wish to use (□ 103). For an Infrastructure connection, the camcorder offers 4 ways to configure an access point and the method you use will depend on the type and specifications of the access point and network you plan to use.

Camera Access Point: When shooting in a location where there are no access points available, the camcorder can serve as a wireless access point*. Wi-Fi enabled devices will be able to connect to the camcorder directly.

* Limited only to the connection between the camcorder and supported Wi-Fi enabled devices. The functionality is not the same as that of commercially available access points.

Infrastructure connection:

WPS (button): If your wireless router supports Wi-Fi Protected Setup (WPS), setup will be easy and require minimal configuring and no passwords. To check if your wireless router has a WPS button and for details about how to activate the Wi-Fi protected setup, refer to the instruction manual of your wireless router.

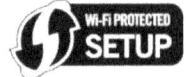

WPS (PIN code): Even if your wireless router does not have a dedicated WPS button, it may support WPS using a PIN code instead. For setup using a PIN code, you will need to know in advance how to activate the wireless router's WPS function. For details refer to the instruction manual of your wireless router.

Searching for Access Points: If your access point does not support the WPS function or you cannot activate it, you can have the camcorder search for access points in the area.

Manual Setup: If the access point you want to use has stealth mode activated and it cannot be automatically detected by the camcorder, you can enter all the necessary settings manually. This requires more advanced knowledge of Wi-Fi and network settings.

IMPORTANT

- Depending on the country/region of use, some restrictions on outdoor use or Camera Access Point connections may apply when operating the IEEE802.11a/n wireless standard in the 5 GHz band. For details about areas of use and restrictions, refer to the *Specifications* (□ 145).

Camera Access Point

In this mode the camcorder itself serves as a wireless access point to which other Wi-Fi-enabled devices can connect. Initially, basic settings for a Camera Access Point connection (network name (SSID): [**GX10-xxxx-xx_Canon0C**], password: [**12345678**]) are already saved under network configuration profile [1:]. You can use the default settings to connect immediately to the camcorder or follow the procedure below if you wish to change the settings.

Operating modes: CAMERA MEDIA | AUTO M

1 **Select [Connection Settings].**

MENU ❯ [🔧 1 System Setup] ❯ [Network Settings] ❯ [Connection Settings]

2 **Select the desired network configuration profile and then select [Camera Access Point].**

Network configuration profile ([1:] to [4:]) ❯ [☰] ❯ [Edit] ❯ [Camera Access Point]

- You can save up to 4 network configuration profiles in the camcorder. If necessary, touch [▲]/[▼] to scroll up/down.

3 **Enter the SSID (network name) the camcorder will use as a Wi-Fi access point.**

[Edit] ❯ Enter the desired network name using the keyboard screen (📖 105) ❯ [OK]

- The network name is needed to connect the network device to the camcorder. If necessary, write it down.

4 **Touch [5 GHz] or [2.4 GHz] to select the frequency band for the Wi-Fi connection.**

5 **Touch [▲] or [▼] to select the desired channel and then touch [OK].**

- Available channels will differ depending on the selected frequency band.

6 **Touch [Open/No encryption] or [WPA2-PSK/AES] to select the encryption method.**

- If you selected [Open/No encryption], skip to step 8.

7 **Enter the encryption key (password).**

[Edit] ❯ Enter the desired password using the keyboard screen (📖 105) ❯ [OK]

- This password is needed to connect the network device to the camcorder. If necessary, write it down.

8 **Continue with the following procedure to configure the IP address assignment (📖 106).**

Using the virtual keyboard screen

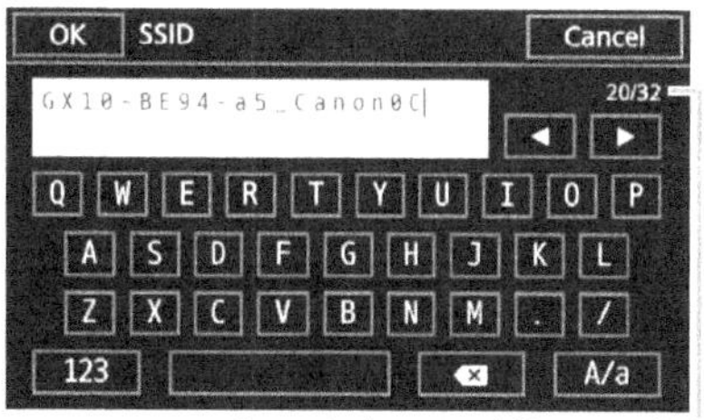

Current character / Character limit

1 Touch the keys on the screen to enter the desired text.
- Touch [◀]/[▶] to change the position of the cursor.
- Touch [123] to switch between letters and numbers/special characters.
- Touch [⌫] to delete the character to the cursor's left.
- Touch [A/a] for caps lock. When the numerical keyboard is displayed, [#%?] switches between set 1 and set 2 of special characters.
- When entering passwords and other sensitive information, the character entered will change to a "●" after a moment to protect the information.

2 After entering the desired text, touch [OK].

Configuring the IP Address Settings

At this point you need to configure the TCP/IP settings. If necessary, consult the network administrator to obtain the relevant information.

1 Touch [Automatic] or [Manual] to select the method for assigning the IP address.
  • If you selected [Automatic], the IP address will be assigned automatically. Continue with the procedure to review and save the configuration (📖 106).

2 To enter the IP address, touch the [≣] button next to [IP Address].
  • Touch [▲] or [▼] to set the value for the first field of the address and then touch the next field to select it. After completing the four fields of the address, touch [OK].

3 Enter the rest of the necessary TCP/IP settings in the same way.
  • Camera Access Point connections: Enter the [Subnet Mask].
  • Infrastructure connections: Enter the [Subnet Mask], [Default Gateway], [Primary DNS Server] and [Secndry DNS Server]. If necessary, touch [▲]/[▼] to scroll up/down.

4 After completing the necessary settings, touch [OK]. Then, with the following procedure to review and save the configuration (📖 106).

Saving the Configuration

1 Review the access point's configuration and then touch [OK].
  • Drag your finger up/down or touch [▲]/[▼] to scroll and review all the information.

2 Enter a name for the new network configuration profile.
  [Edit] ❯ Enter the desired name using the keyboard screen (📖 105) ❯ [OK]
  • If you wish, you can give the network configuration profile a more descriptive name to make it easier to identify.

3 Touch [OK] to save the network configuration profile.
  • If you selected a network configuration profile that contained previous settings, these will be overwritten with the new configuration you reviewed in step 1.

4 When the confirmation message appears, touch [OK] and then touch [✕].

Connecting in Infrastructure Mode

Operating modes: CAMERA MEDIA | AUTO M

1 Select [Connection Settings].
  MENU ❯ [❤ ① System Setup] ❯ [Network Settings] ❯ [Connection Settings]

2 Select the desired network configuration profile and then select [Infrastructure].
  Network configuration profile ([1:] to [4:]) ❯ [≣] ❯ [Edit] ❯ [Infrastructure]
  • You can save up to 4 network configuration profiles in the camcorder. If necessary, touch [▲]/[▼] to scroll up/down.

3 Touch one of the buttons to select the desired network setup method.
  • Continue the setup with the procedure corresponding to the method you wish to use (see the reference pages below).
  [WPS: Button] (📖 107)
  [WPS: PIN Code] (📖 107)
  [Search for Access Points] (📖 108)
  [Manual] (📖 109)

Wi-Fi Protected Setup (WPS)

Wi-Fi Protected Setup (WPS) is the easiest way to set up a Wi-Fi access point. You can do simply by pushing a button (if the access point (wireless router) you want to connect to has a WPS button) or using a PIN code issued by the camcorder.

Wireless Routers with a WPS Button

1 Press and hold the WPS button on the wireless router.

- The length of time required to hold down the WPS button depends on the wireless router. Refer to the instruction manual of your wireless router and make sure the wireless router's WPS function is activated.

2 Within 2 minutes, touch [OK].

- While [Connecting] appears on the screen, you can touch [Cancel] to cancel the operation.

3 Continue with the procedure to configure the IP address assignment (□ 106).

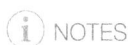 NOTES

- The [WPS: Button] method may not work correctly if there are several active access points in the area. In such case try using [WPS: PIN Code] or [Search for Access Points] (□ 108) instead.

WPS Using a PIN Code

1 After you select [WPS: PIN Code], the camcorder will generate and display an 8-digit PIN code on the screen.

2 Enter the PIN code into the wireless router's WPS (PIN code) setup screen.

- For most wireless routers, you must use a Web browser to access the setup screen.
- For details about how to access your wireless router's settings and activate the Wi-Fi Protected Setup (WPS) using a PIN code, refer to the instruction manual of your wireless router.

3 Within 2 minutes, touch [OK].

- While [Connecting] appears on the screen, you can touch [Cancel] to cancel the operation.
- After the connection is correctly established, the previous menu screen will appear again on the screen.

4 Continue with the procedure to configure the IP address assignment (□ 106).

Searching for Access Points

The camcorder will automatically detect access points in the vicinity. After you select the desired access point, you only need to enter the selected network's password to connect the camcorder. For details about the access point's network name (SSID) and password, refer to the wireless router's instruction manual or consult the network administrator in charge of the access point.

Network name (SSID)　　　　　　　　Encrypted access point

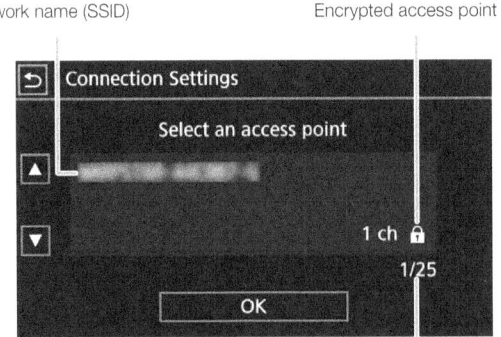

Current access point/Total number
of active access points detected

1 After you select [Search for Access Points], the camcorder will search for active access points in the vicinity and display a list of available options on the screen.

2 Touch the desired access point.
- Drag your finger up/down or touch [▲]/[▼] to scroll up/down.
- If the access point is not encrypted (🔒 icon is not displayed), continue with the procedure to configure the IP address assignment (🔲 106).

3 If necessary (depending on the access point's encryption), touch one of the buttons to select the WEP index.

4 Enter the encryption key (password).
[Edit] ❯ Enter the password using the keyboard screen (🔲 105) ❯ [OK]

5 Continue with the procedure to configure the IP address assignment (🔲 106).

Manual Setup

If you prefer, you can enter manually the details of the Wi-Fi network you want to connect to. Follow the instructions on the screen to complete the procedure.

1 Enter the access point's SSID (network name).

[Edit] ❯ Enter the network name using the keyboard screen (📖 105) ❯ [OK]

2 Select the authentication method.

- If you selected [Open], touch [WEP] and continue the procedure, or touch [No encryption] and continue with the procedure to configure the IP address assignment (📖 106).

3 Select the WEP index or encryption method, depending on the selected authentication mode.

- [Shared Key]/[WEP]: Touch one of the buttons to select the WEP index.
- [WPA-PSK]/[WPA2-PSK]: Touch [TKIP] or [AES].

4 Enter the encryption key (password).

[Edit] ❯ Enter the password using the keyboard screen (📖 105) ❯ [OK]

5 Continue with the procedure to configure the IP address assignment (📖 106).

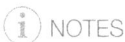 NOTES

Valid passwords vary depending on the encryption method.

64-bit WEP encryption: 5 ASCII characters or 10 hexadecimal characters.

128-bit WEP encryption: 13 ASCII characters or 26 hexadecimal characters.

AES / TKIP encryption: 8 to 63 ASCII characters or 64 hexadecimal characters.

* Note: ASCII characters include the numbers 0 to 9, the letters a to z and A to Z and some punctuation marks and special symbols. Hexadecimal characters comprise the numbers 0 to 9 and the letters a to f and A to F.

Selecting a Network Connection and Changing Network Settings

Operating modes: [CAMERA] [MEDIA] | [AUTO] [M]

Selecting a Network Connection

You can save up to 4 network configuration profiles. If you just saved a new network configuration, it will already be automatically selected so follow this procedure to select a different configuration profile.

1 Select [Connection Settings].

MENU ❯❯ [𝗬 ① System Setup] ❯❯ [Network Settings] ❯❯ [Connection Settings]

2 Select the desired network configuration profile.

Network configuration profile ([1:] to [4:]) ❯❯ [↺] ❯❯ [✖]

Changing Network Settings

You can check and, if necessary, edit the settings of the currently selected network configuration profile even after the initial setup. Changing settings manually requires more advanced knowledge of Wi-Fi and network settings.

1 Select [Connection Settings].

MENU ❯❯ [𝗬 ① System Setup] ❯❯ [Network Settings] ❯❯ [Connection Settings]

2 Select the desired network configuration profile.

Network configuration profile ([1:] to [4:]) ❯❯ [⊞]

- The current network settings will be displayed. Drag your finger up/down or touch [▲]/[▼] to scroll and review all the information.

3 To change the network settings, touch [Edit] and then [Infrastructure] or [Camera Access Point].

- Change the network settings as described in the previous sections.
  Infrastrucure connections (📖 106, from step 3)
  Camera Access Point connections (📖 105, from step 3)

Browser Remote: Controlling the Camcorder from a Network Device

After connecting the camcorder to a Wi-Fi network, you can operate the camcorder remotely via Browser Remote, a Web browser application that can be accessed using the Web browser on network devices*. Using Browser Remote, you can check the camcorder's live view image and control various recording settings. On the Browser Remote screen, you can also check the remaining recording time on the SD card, remaining battery charge and the camcorder's time code.

* For details about compatible devices, operating systems, Web browsers, etc., please visit your local Canon website.

Setting Up Browser Remote

You can set a unique camcorder identification code and designate the port that the Browser Remote application should use when accessing the camcorder through the network. The port number (HTTP protocol) used by Browser Remote is usually set to port 80, but you can change it if necessary. The camcorder ID will appear on the Browser Remote screen, making it easy to identify which camcorder the application is controlling in case of a multi-camera shooting setup.

Operating modes: [CAMERA] | [AUTO] [M]

1 Select [Browser Remote Settings].

   MENU ❯❯ [❡ 1 System Setup] ❯❯ [Network Settings] ❯❯ [Browser Remote Settings]

2 To change the port number, touch the [☰] button next to [Port No.].

   • Touch [▲] or [▼] to set the value for the first digit of the port number and then touch the next digit to select it. After completing all the digits of the port number, touch [OK].

3 Enter the camcorder ID.

   • [Edit] ❯❯ Enter the desired text using the keyboard screen (□ 105) ❯❯ [OK]

4 Touch [↩] and then touch [✕].

Starting Browser Remote

After completing the network connection, you can start the Browser Remote application on the Web browser* of any network device** connected to the same network.

* A Web browser that supports JavaScript and is enabled to accept cookies is required.
**For details about compatible devices, operating systems, Web browsers, etc., please visit your local Canon website.

Operating modes: [CAMERA] | [AUTO] [M]

Preparations on the Camcorder

1 Select the desired network connection (囗 110).
  • Use a Camera Access Point connection.

2 Activate the Browser Remote function.
  MENU ❯ [❨ ① System Setup] ❯ [Network Settings] ❯ [Activate] ❯ [Browser Remote]
  • The camcorder will start functioning as a wireless access point.
  • The connection type icon and Remote will appear at the right of the screen. When the icons turn white, the camcorder is ready to accept commands from the Browser Remote application.

3 If necessary, display the camcorder's settings to complete the connection.
  [↩] ❯ [View Information]
  • The current Browser Remote and network settings will be displayed. If necessary, touch [▲]/[▼] to scroll up/down.
  • You will need the camcorder's SSID (network name) to connect a Wi-Fi device using a Camera Access Point connection. You will need the camcorder's URL to use the Browser Remote application.

4 Touch [↩] and then [✕] to close the menu.

On the Network Device

1 Connect the network device to the camcorder.
  • On Wi-Fi devices select the camcorder's SSID (network name) in the Wi-Fi settings.

2 Start the Web browser on the network device.

3 Enter the camcorder's URL exactly as shown on the camcorder's information screen.

http://192.168.0.80

  • The Browser Remote screen will appear.
  • While Browser Remote is correctly connected to the camcorder, the network connection indicator's ●●●● will keep turning on and off in a loop.
  • If the camcorder's ID was set, it will appear on the Browser Remote screen while live view is not activated.

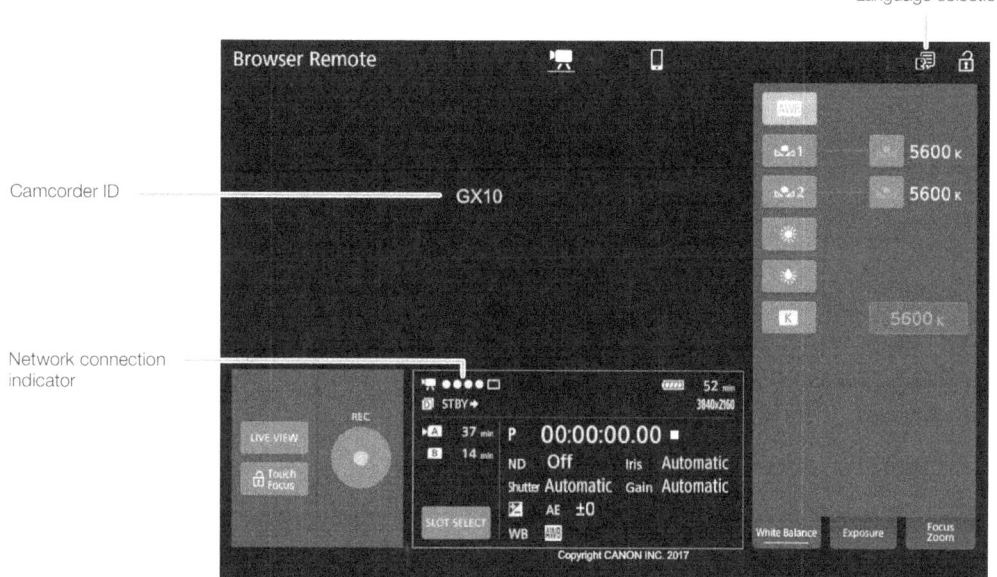

Language selection

Camcorder ID

Network connection indicator

4 Select the language for Browser Remote.
  • Touch the language selection icon and select the desired language from the list. The language selected applies mainly to the messages displayed in the application. The application's buttons are displayed in English only, regardless of the language selected.

5 Use the Browser Remote controls to operate the camcorder.
  • Descriptions of the controls are given in the following pages. Detailed operation is given in each function's reference page.

6 When you have finished using Browser Remote, turn it off on the camcorder.
  MENU ❯ [✚ 1 System Setup] ❯ [Network Settings] ❯ [Activate] ❯ [Off]
  • The network icons will turn yellow and then disappear from the screen and the connection with the application will be terminated.

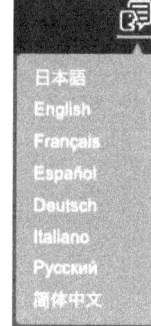

(i) NOTES

• The live view image will not be displayed in Browser Remote while color bars are displayed on the camcorder.
• Depending on the network used and the strength of the Wi-Fi signal, you may notice delays in the refreshing of the live view image and other settings.
• If Browser Remote is set to a language other than the language used on the network device, the application may not be displayed correctly.

Using Browser Remote

The Browser Remote application has 2 screens. The main screen, ['🎥'], is used for controlling the camcorder remotely in recording mode. The basic screen, [🔲], allows users only to zoom or start/stop recording using a smartphone or other device with a small screen.

The following sections explain how to use the Browser Remote controls. For detailed information and applicable restrictions about the functions themselves, please refer to each function's explanation.

(i) NOTES

• Browser Remote does not support multi-touch gestures.

The Main Remote Recording Screen ['🎥']

When using a computer, tablet and other devices with larger screens, this screen offers all the controls available for operating the camcorder remotely via Browser Remote.

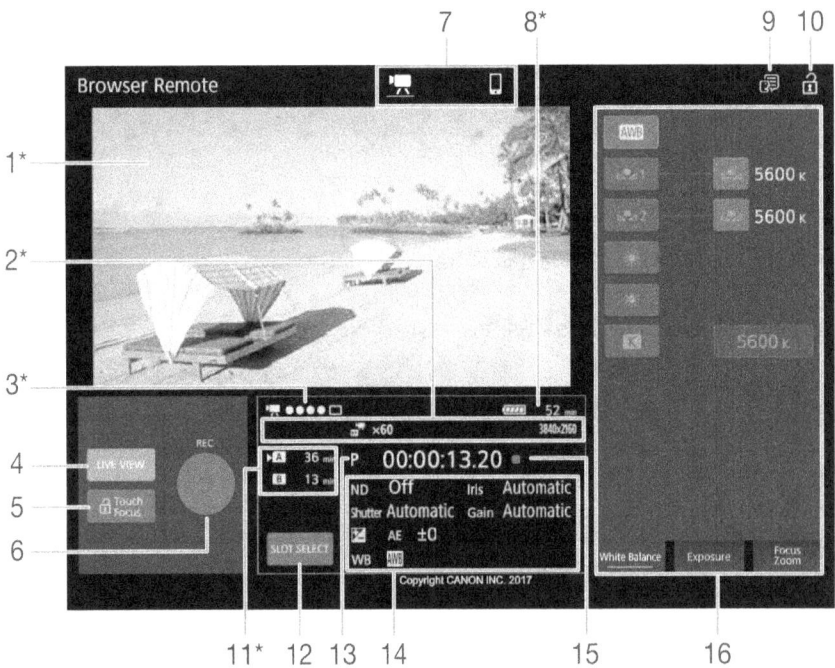

* Onscreen display/indication only. The content or value cannot be changed using Browser Remote.

1   Live view screen

Shows the camcorder's live view image. When the live view image is not turned on, the camcorder ID will appear here. The camcorder's live view image will not be displayed when the camcorder is set to internal recording with a video configuration of 3840x2160 at 59.94P (□ 42), and [☑ Display Setup] ❯ [HDMI Max Resolution] is set to [3840x2160] (□ 100).

2   Information about the recording

🔳 :	Dual recording (□ 43).
STBY ➡ , REC ➡ :	Recording command (□ 99).
🔳, 🔳 :	Slow & fast motion recording (□ 44).
🔳 :	Pre-recording (□ 80).
0000x0000:	Resolution (□ 42).

3   Connection indicator

While Browser Remote is correctly connected to the camcorder, the dots will keep turning on and off in a loop.

4   [LIVE VIEW] button

Touch the button to display the camcorder's live view image on the Browser Remote screen.

5   [🔒 Touch Focus] button

Touch the button to unlock (enable) the touch focus mode.

6   [REC] button

Touch the button to start recording. While recording, the center of the button turns red.

Touch the button again to stop recording.

7   Browser Remote screen selection

Touch ['🎥] to open the main remote recording screen or [📱] to open the basic screen for devices with a small screen (📖 118).

8   Remaining battery charge (📖 39)

9   Language selection (📖 113)

10 Key lock button

Touch the icon to lock the Browser Remote screens in order to prevent settings from being changed inadvertently.

11 SD cards and approximate remaining recording time

The currently selected SD card is indicated with a ▶ mark next to the icon.

Remaining recording times are approximate and calculated based on the current video configuration used.

12 [SLOT SELECT] button

Touch the button to select the other SD card when both SD card slots contain a card.

13 Shooting mode (📖 58) / AUTO mode (📖 26)

When the camcorder is set to AUTO mode, the shooting mode cannot be selected.

14 Current camcorder settings

This panel displays an overview of the camcorder settings currently used. You can change these settings with the controls in the detailed camcorder settings panel (16) on the right.

[ND]: ND filter	[WB]: White balance
[Shutter]: Shutter speed	[Iris]: Aperture value
[Z]: Exposure compensation	[Gain]: Gain value

15 Time code (📖 68) and recording operation (📖 39) (same as on the camcorder)

16 Detailed camcorder settings panel (📖 116)

Touch one of the tabs at the bottom to select the camcorder settings you wish to adjust:

[White Balance]:	White balance mode and related settings.
[Exposure]:	Exposure related settings—aperture, shutter speed and gain.
[Focus	Zoom]:	Focus related settings and zoom operations.

The Main Remote Recording Screen: Detailed Camcorder Settings

The following sections explain how to use the controls in the detailed camcorder settings panel. For detailed information and applicable restrictions about the functions themselves, please refer to each function's explanation.

To change the white balance
Touch the [White Balance] tab in the detailed camcorder settings panel.

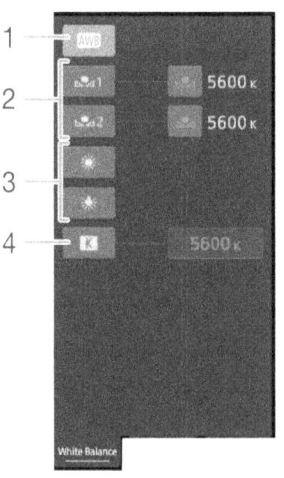

1   Automatic white balance button

Touch [AWB] to set the camcorder to auto white balance (AWB) mode.

2   Custom white balance buttons

Touch [◻1] or [◻2].

To register a custom white balance: Point the camcorder at a gray card or white object with no pattern so it fills the center of the live view screen and touch [◻]. Use the same lighting conditions you plan to use when recording.

During the procedure, the icon in the button will flash quickly. When it stops flashing, the procedure is completed and the custom white balance will be applied.

3   Preset white balance settings

Touch [☀] or [☀].

4   Color temperature setting

Touch [K]. Touch the color temperature button on the right, select the desired value from the list and then touch [✕].

To change exposure-related settings
Touch the [Exposure] tab in the detailed camcorder settings panel.

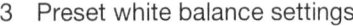

1   [Mode] (shooting mode) button

Touch the button, touch the icon of the desired shooting mode (□ 58) and then touch [✕].

2   ND Filter buttons

- Touch [–] or [+] to change the density of the ND filter (displayed above the buttons). You can also touch the current ND filter setting, select the desired setting from the list (or touch [–]/[+]) and then touch [✕].

3   Aperture related buttons

- Touch [–] or [+] to change the aperture value (displayed above the buttons). You can also touch the current aperture value, select the desired value from the list (or touch [–]/[+]) and then touch [✕].

4   Shutter speed related buttons

- Touch [–] or [+] to change the shutter speed (displayed above the buttons). You can also touch the current shutter speed value, select the desired value from the list (or touch [–]/[+]) and then touch [✕].

5   Gain related buttons

- Touch [–] or [+] to change the gain value (displayed above the buttons). You can also touch the current gain value, select the desired value from the list (or touch [–]/[+]) and then touch [✕].

6   Exposure adjustment buttons

Touch [–] or [+] to compensate the exposure. You can also touch the current exposure compensation value, select the desired value from the list (or touch [–]/[+]) and then touch [✕].

If necessary, touch [✳] to lock the exposure.

To adjust the focus and use focus-related functions
Touch the [Focus | Zoom] tab in the detailed camcorder settings panel.

1 Focus mode button

2 [Focus Guide] (Dual Pixel Focus Guide function) button

3 Manual focus buttons

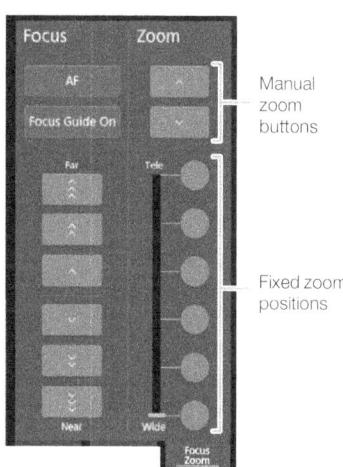

Manual focus

1 Touch the focus mode button, touch [MF] and then touch [✕].

  • Touch [AF] to return the camcorder to continuous AF.

2 Touch one of the manual focus buttons on the [Near] side to focus closer or one of the buttons on the [Far] side to focus farther away. There are three levels of adjustment - [⌃]/[⌄] is the smallest and [⌃̂]/[⌄̌] the largest.

Focus guide

1 In manual focus mode, touch the [Focus Guide Off] button.

2 Touch [On] to display the focus guide (□ 46) and then touch [✕].

Touch focus

In autofocus mode, you can touch on a subject that appears in the Browser Remote's live view screen in order to select it for focusing.

1 Make sure the touch focus function has been unlocked and the 🔓 icon appears in the button (□ 115).

2 Touch the desired subject in the live view screen.

  • Depending on the focus mode used, an AF frame will appear on the selected subject.

Adjusting the zoom

Touch the [Focus | Zoom] tab in the detailed camcorder settings panel.

1 Touch one of the fixed zoom position buttons on the [Tele] side to zoom in or one of the buttons on the [Wide] side to zoom out.

  • You can also touch the manual zoom buttons [⌃]/[⌄].

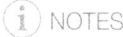

Manual zoom buttons

Fixed zoom positions

(i) NOTES

• When using a slow zoom speed, it may take some time until the lens starts moving.

The Basic Screen [▯]

When using a smartphone or other device with a smaller screen, this screen offers only a small live image screen for final confirmation, zoom controls and the [REC] button to start and stop recording.

To open the basic screen, touch the [▯] icon at the top of the Browser Remote screen.

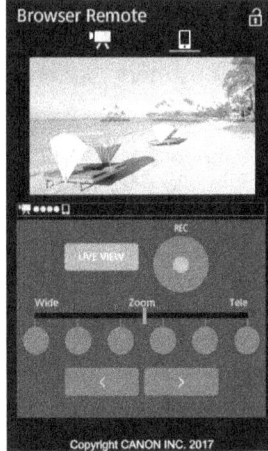

FTP File Transfer

You can transfer clips from the camcorder to another device connected to the network, using the FTP protocol. The following explanations assume that the FTP server is on, ready and correctly configured.

Operating modes: MEDIA

Setting Up the FTP Server and Transfer Settings

Before you can transfer clips to a connected device, you need to configure the FTP server settings and other settings related to the handling of folders and files. If necessary, consult the network administrator in charge of the FTP server.

1 Select [FTP Transfer Settings].

MENU ▶ [🔧 1 System Setup] ▶ [Network Settings] ▶ [FTP Transfer Settings]

2 To enter the destination FTP server, touch the [☰] button next to [FTP Server].

[Edit] ▶ Enter the desired text (IP address or host name) using the keyboard screen (📖 105) ▶ [OK]

3 Enter the [FTP: User Name], [FTP: Password], and [Destination Folder] in the same way.

4 To enter the FTP port number, touch the [☰] button next to [Port No.].

- Touch [▲] or [▼] to set the value for the first digit of the port number and then touch the next digit to select it. After completing all the digits of the port number, touch [OK].

5 Select whether to activate the passive mode.

[☰] button next to [Passive Mode] ▶ [On] or [Off] ▶ [↶]

- [Off] is the standard setting for most cases. [On] (passive mode) is more appropriate for FTP transfers within a network behind a firewall.

6 Select whether to create a new folder for every recording date.

[☰] button next to [New Folder by Date] ▶ [On] or [Off] ▶ [↶]

7 Select how to handle file transfers when a file with the same name already exists on the server.

[☰] button next to [Same Named Files] ▶ Desired option ▶ [↶]

8 Touch [↶] and the touch [✕].

ⓘ NOTES

- If necessary, you can check the current FTP server and FTP transfer settings with the [🔧 1 System Setup] ▶ [Network Settings] ▶ [View Information] setting.

Options for [New Folder by Date]

[On]:	A new subfolder under the transfer destination folder "YYYYMMDD\HHMMSS" will be created for every transfer operation.
[Off]:	All the files will be transferred to the folder set as [Destination Folder] in the FTP server settings.

Options for [Same Named Files]

[Overwrite]:	Even if a file with the same name already exists in the destination folder, the file will be transferred, overwriting any file with the same name in the destination folder.
[Skip]:	If a file with the same name already exists in the destination folder, the file will not be transferred.

Transferring Clips (FTP Transfer)

1 Select the desired network connection (🕮 110).
* Use an Infrastructure connection.

2 Open the desired clip index screen (🕮 89).

3 Select [FTP Transfer].

[FUNC] ❯ [FTP Transfer]

4 Touch the desired option and then touch [Yes].

* When you select [Select], perform the following procedure to select the individual clips you want to transfer before touching [Yes].
* When the connection to the FTP server is completed, all the applicable clips will be transferred to the FTP server.
* Touch [Stop] to interrupt the operation while it is in progress. The operation will stop after the current file is transferred.

5 When the confirmation message appears, touch [OK].

To select individual clips

1 Touch on the individual clips you want to transfer.

* A checkmark ✓ will appear on the clips you touch. The total number of selected clips will appear next to the 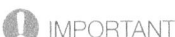 icon.
* Touch a selected clip to remove the checkmark. To remove all checkmarks at once, touch [Remove All] ❯ [Yes].

2 After selecting all the desired clips, touch [OK].

Options

[Select]:   You can select the individual clips you want to transfer.

[All Clips]:   Transfers all the clips.

🔅 IMPORTANT

* Observe the following precautions when transferring files. Failing to do so may interrupt the transfer and incomplete files may remain at the transfer destination.
  - Do not open the SD card compartment cover.
  - Do not disconnect the power source or turn off the camcorder.
* If incomplete files remain at the transfer destination, check the content and make sure they are safe to delete before deleting them.

ⓘ NOTES

* Depending on the access point's settings and capabilities, it may take some time to transfer files.

Menu Options

For details about how to select an item, refer to *Using the Menus* (□ 32). For details about each function, see the reference page. Setting options in boldface indicate default values. Depending on the camcorder's operating mode and other current settings, some menu items may not be available. Such menu items do not appear or appear grayed out in menu screens.

To skip directly to the page of a specific menu:

FUNC Menu

FUNC menu (CAMERA mode)

Menu item	Setting options and additional information	
[IRIS Aperture]	Aperture value adjustment dial, F2.8 to F11; Zebra pattern button*: [⬛OFF **Off**], [⬛70 70%], [⬛100 100%]	(□ 59)
[SHTR Shutter Speed]	Shutter speed adjustment dial, 1/8 (59.94P or 29.97P frame rate) or 1/6 (23.98P frame rate only) to 1/2000; Zebra pattern button*: [⬛OFF **Off**], [⬛70 70%], [⬛100 100%]	(□ 58)
[GAIN Gain]	Gain value adjustment dial, 0.0 dB to 39.0 dB; Zebra pattern button*: [⬛OFF **Off**], [⬛70 70%], [⬛100 100%]	(□ 59)
[GAIN AGC Limit]	[**M**] (set a limit): Turn on/off (**off**), when [**M**] is on – AGC limit adjustment dial, 0.0 dB to 38.0 dB ([**0.0db**]).	(□ 57)
[☑ Exposure Comp.]	Touch AE frame, [⊞] (Touch AE settings): [N Normal], [H Highlights]; Zebra pattern button*: [⬛OFF **Off**], [⬛70 70%], [⬛100 100%]; [✱] (AE lock): Turn on/off (**off**), when [✱] is on – exposure compensation adjustment dial ([**AE ±0**]).	(□ 61)
[White Balance]*	[**AWB Automatic**], [☀ Daylight], [💡 Tungsten], [K Color Temperature], [⬝ Set 1], [⬝ Set 2]; [⊞] (additional settings): color temperature adjustment dial[1] ([**5600K**]) or [Set WB] to register a custom white balance setting[2]. [1] Only when [K Color Temperature] is selected. [2] Only when [⬝ Set 1] or [⬝ Set 2] is selected.	(□ 65)
[BLC Always On]*	[⬛OFF **Off**], [⬛ On]	(□ 62)
[⊙ Focus]	[**A Automatic**], [M Manual], when [M] is selected – focus preset button; Touch AF frame; [⊞] (peaking settings): [Peaking and B&W], [Peaking Color], [PEAK] (peaking): Turn on/off (**off**).	(□ 45)
[MAGN. Magnification]	[OK] (display magnified screen)	(□ 48)
[ZOOM Zoom]	Onscreen zoom controls, [PHOTO] (take a photo), [REC]/[STOP] (record a clip); [⬝]/[⬝OFF] (tracking): Turn on/off (**off**); [2.0x] (digital tele-converter): Turn on/off (**off**).	(□ 55)

Menu item	Setting options and additional information	
[Looks]*	[✿1 **Standard**], [✿2 Wide DR], [✿3 Monochrome]; [▦] [3] (fine adjustment): [Sharpness], [Contrast], [Color Depth].	(🕮 67)
	[3] Available options, default values and adjustment ranges vary depending on the current [Looks] setting.	
[♪)) Audio]	Audio levels for audio channels CH1 and CH2; [🎤A **Automatic**], [🎤M Manual], when [🎤M Manual] is selected – Audio level adjustment [◀], [▶]: 00 to 100 **(50)**.;	(🕮 74)
	[♪STD]* (audio scene): [♪STD **Standard**], [♪ Music], [🎪 Festival], [👤 Speech], [🎙 Meeting], [🌲 Forest and Birds], [🔇 Noise Suppression], [♪c Custom Setting]	(🕮 72)

* The button shows the icon of the current setting.

FUNC menu (MEDIA mode)

Menu item	Setting options and additional information		
For clips:	[📹] index screen	Single clip (playback pause)	
[Copy (Ⓐ ➔ Ⓑ)], [Copy (Ⓑ ➔ Ⓐ)]	<folder name>,	—	(🕮 95)
[Delete]	[Select], [All Clips]	●	(🕮 93)
[FTP Transfer]	[Select], [All Clips]	—	(🕮 120)
[Trim]	—	●	(🕮 94)
For photos:	[📷] index screen	Single photo view	
[Copy (Ⓐ ➔ Ⓑ)], [Copy (Ⓑ ➔ Ⓐ)]	<folder name>,	—	(🕮 95)
[Delete]	[Select], [All Photos]	●	(🕮 93)

Setup Menus

['🎥 Camera Setup] menu (CAMERA mode only)

Menu item	Setting options and additional information	
[Digital Zoom]	[**Off** Off], [30× Advanced], [300× 300x], [2.0× Digital Tele-conv.]	
	Determines the operation of the digital zoom. The color of the zoom indicator indicates the zoom ratio. • With the digital zoom the image is digitally processed, so the image resolution will deteriorate the more you zoom in. • This setting is not available when [Conversion Lens] is set to [Wide WA-U58]. • [30× Advanced] is not available in the following cases: - When [🎬 Recording Setup] ❯ [Resolution] is set to [3840x2160 (150 Mbps)]. - When [🎬 Recording Setup] ❯ [Resolution] is set to [1920x1080 (35 Mbps)] or [1920x1080 (17 Mbps)], slow & fast recording is activated and the slow motion rate is set to 0.5x (59.94P)	
[Zoom Speed Level]	[≫ Fast], [≫ **Normal**], [≫ Slow]	(🕮 53, 54)
[Zoom Rocker Zoom Speed]	[VAR] **(variable speed)**, [CONST] (constant speed), when [CONST] is selected – Zoom speed adjustment bar: 1 to 16 **(8)**	(🕮 53)
[Wireless Ctrlr Zoom Speed]	Zoom speed adjustment bar: 1 to 16 **(8)**	(🕮 54)
[High-Speed Zoom]	[**On** On], [**Off** Off]	(🕮 54)
[AF Mode]	[BOOST AF-Boosted MF], [CONT **Continuous**]	(🕮 48, 49)
[AF Frame Size]	[**A** Automatic], [**L** Large], [**S** Small]	(🕮 49)
[AF Speed]	[≫ Fast], [≫ **Normal**], [≫ Slow]	(🕮 50)

Menu item	Setting options and additional information	
[AF Response]	[▶▶ Fast], [▶▶ **Normal**], [▶ Slow]	(□ 50)
[Face Detection & Tracking]	[**ON On** ☺], [**OFF** Off]	(□ 50)
[Focus Guide]	[**ON On**], [**OFF** Off]	(□ 46)
[Focus Preset Speed]	[▶▶ Fast], [▶▶ **Normal**], [▶ Slow]	(□ 46)
	Determines the speed at which the focus changes to the preset position.	
[Auto Backlight Correction]	[**ON On**], [**OFF** Off]	(□ 62)
[Auto Slow Shutter]	[**ON On**], [**OFF** Off]	
	The camcorder automatically uses slow shutter speeds to obtain brighter recordings in places with insufficient lighting. • When this setting is set to [**ON** On], the fastest shutter speed used is: 1/30 (59.94P), 1/5 (29.97P) or 1/12 (23.98P). • Auto slow shutter can be activated only during AUTO mode or when the shooting mode is set to **P**. • If a trailing afterimage appears, set the auto slow shutter to [**OFF** Off].	
[Conversion Lens]	[**Tele** TL-U58], [**Wide** WA-U58], [**OFF** Off]	
	When you attach to the camcorder the optional TL-U58 Tele-converter or WA-U58 Wide Attachment, set the appropriate conversion lens setting. The image stabilization method and minimum focusing distance will change according to the accessory used. The minimum focusing distance throughout the entire zoom range will be 130 cm (4 ft. 3 in.) for the tele-converter and about 60 cm (2 ft.) for the wide attachment. • The tele-converter increases the focal length of the lens by a factor of approx. 1.5. The wide attachment reduces the focal length of the lens by a factor of approx. 0.8. • The approximate focusing distance displayed on the screen will change depending on the setting. If you are not using an optional conversion lens, select [**OFF** Off]. • When a setting other than [**OFF** Off] is selected, the ['🎥 Camera Setup] ❯ [AF Mode] setting will not be available.	
[Image Stabilizer]	[(❲❳)OFF Off], [((❤)) **Standard**], [(❤)D Dynamic]	(□ 56)
[Powered IS Button]	[**ON** Press and Hold], [**ON/OFF** Toggle On/Off]	
	Determines the operation mode of the POWERED IS button (□ 56). [**ON** Press and Hold]: Powered IS will be activated while you hold the button pressed down. [**ON/OFF** Toggle On/Off]: Each press of the button will turn the Powered IS function on and off.	
[Set WB Priority]	[**AWB** Automatic], [☀ Daylight], [☀ Tungsten], [**K** Color Temperature], [.◢ Set 1], [.◢ Set 2]	
	You can press an assignable button set to [**WB** WB Priority] to switch between the current white balance and the white balance setting selected for [Set WB Priority].	
[Focus Ring Direction]	[**NORM** Normal], [**REV** Reverse]	
	Changes the direction the focus/zoom ring needs to be turned when using it to adjust the focus (when the focus/zoom ring switch is set to FOCUS).	
[Focus Ring Response]	[▶▶ Fast], [▶▶ **Normal**], [▶ Slow]	
	Selects the sensitivity of the response when operating the focus/zoom ring. This setting affects the focus/zoom ring only when using it to adjust the focus (when the focus/zoom ring switch is set to FOCUS).	
[Zoom Ring Direction]	[**NORM** Normal], [**REV** Reverse]	
	Changes the direction the focus/zoom ring needs to be turned when using it to adjust the zoom (when the focus/zoom ring switch is set to ZOOM).	

[▶ Playback Setup] menu ([MEDIA] mode only)

Menu item	Setting options and additional information
[MP4 Data Code]	[OFF Off], [📅 Date]
[📷 Data Code]	[OFF Off], [📅 Date], [⊘ Time], [📅⊘ Date and Time], [📷 Camera Data]
	Displays the date when a clip was recorded ([MP4 Data Code]) or the date and/or time when a photo was recorded ([📷 Data Code]).

[🎥 Recording Setup] menu

Menu item	Setting options and additional information	
[Internal/External Rec]	['🎥 Internal Rec Priority], [HDMI External Rec Only (HDMI)]	(📖 42, 99)
[Resolution]	[3840x2160 (150 Mbps)], [1920x1080 (35 Mbps)], [1920x1080 (17 Mbps)], [1280x720 (8 Mbps)], [1280x720 (4 Mbps)]	(📖 42)
[Frame Rate]	[59.94P 59.94P], [29.97P 29.97P], [23.98P 23.98P]	(📖 42)
[Recording Media]	['🎥 Rec Media for Movies]: [A Mem. Card A], [B Mem. Card B] [📷 Rec Media for Photos]: [A Mem. Card A], [B Mem. Card B]	(📖 31)
[Dual/Relay Recording]	['🎥 Standard Recording], [D Dual Recording], [A↷ Relay Recording] (or [B↷ Relay Recording])	(📖 43)
[Slow & Fast Motion]	[OFF Off], [x0.2], [x0.25], [x0.4], [x0.5], [x0.8], [x2], [x4], [x10], [x20], [x60], [x120], [x600], [x1200]	(📖 44)
[Available Space in Memory], [Used Space in Memory]	[A] (SD card A), [B] (SD card B)	
	Displays a screen where you can check the total space available on the SD card and the SD card's speed class. In [CAMERA] mode, the screen shows also the available space on the card and an estimate of the remaining recording time (MP4) and the remaining number of photos (📷), based on current settings. In [MEDIA] mode, the screen shows also the amount of space currently used by recordings.	
[Initialize SD]	[A Mem. Card A], [B Mem. Card B]	(📖 31)
[External Rec Video Config.]	[3840x2160 59.94P YCC420 8bit][1], [1920x1080 59.94P YCC422 10bit], [3840x2160 29.97P YCC422 8bit][1], [1920x1080 29.97P YCC422 10bit]	(📖 99)
	[1] Only when [🎥 Recording Setup] ▶ [Internal/External Rec] is set to [HDMI External Rec Only (HDMI)].	
[Rec Command]	[ON On], [OFF Off]	(📖 99)
[HDMI Time Code]	[ON On], [OFF Off]	
	When this setting is set to [ON On], the HDMI signal output from the camcorder includes the camcorder's time code.	
[Time Code Mode]	[PRESET Preset], [REGEN. Regen.]	(📖 68)
[Time Code Running Mode]	[RECRUN Rec Run], [FREERUN Free Run]	(📖 68)
[DF/NDF]	[DF DF], [NDF NDF]	(📖 69)
[Initial Time Code]	Time code input screen (00:00:00:00 to 23:59:59:29)	(📖 68)
[User Bit Type]	[SET Setting], [TIME Time], [DATE Date]; when [SET Setting] is selected – [☰]: user bit input screen (00 00 00 00 to FF FF FF FF).	(📖 70)
[Color Bars]	[OFF Off], [SMPTE SMPTE], [ARIB ARIB]	(📖 79)
[1 kHz Tone]	[-12dB –12 dB], [-18dB –18 dB], [-20dB –20 dB], [OFF Off]	(📖 79)

Menu item	Setting options and additional information
[File Numbering]	[🔄 Reset], [➡ **Continuous**]

MP4 clips and photos are saved as files in folders. You can select the file numbering method for those files. File numbers appear on screens in playback mode in a format such as "101-0107". The first 3 digits indicate the folder number and the last 4 digits are different for each file in a folder.

[🔄 Reset]: File numbers will restart from 100-0001 every time you insert a new (or initialized) SD card. If the card already contains previous recordings, file numbers will continue from the number following that of the last recording on the SD card.

[➡ Continuous]: File numbers will continue from the number following that of the last file recorded with the camcorder. This setting is the most convenient for managing files on a computer. We recommend using the [➡ Continuous] setting.

Understanding folder names
- An example folder name is "101_1103". The first 3 digits indicate the folder number (from 100 to 999) and the last 4 digits indicate the month and day when the folder was created. In the example, the folder numbered 101 was created on November 3.
- Each folder can contain up to 500 files (MP4 clips and photos combined). When that number is exceeded, a new folder is created automatically.

Understanding file numbers
- An example file number is "101-0107". The first 3 digits indicate the folder number where the clip/photo is stored and the last 4 digits indicate the consecutive number assigned to the recording (from 0001 to 9999).
- The file number also indicates the name and location of the file on the SD card. For example, an MP4 clip numbered 101-0107 that was recorded on November 3, is located in the "DCIM**101**_1103" folder as the file "MVI_**0107**.MP4"; a photo with the same file number will be saved in the same folder as the file "IMG_**0107**.JPG".

[♪)) Audio Setup] menu

Menu item	Setting options and additional information	
[Built-in Mic Att.]	[**ON** On], [**OFF** Off]	(📖 74)
[Built-in Mic Wind Screen]	[H **Auto (High)**], [L Auto (Low) ≥/●], [**OFF** Off ≥/●]	(📖 75)
[Built-in Mic Freq. Response]	[**NORM** **Normal**], [**LB** Boost LF Range], [**LC** Low Cut Filter], [**MB** Boost MF Range], [**LHB** Boost HF+LF Range]	(📖 75)
[Built-in Mic Directionality]	[**2ch MONO** Monaural], [**NORM** **Normal**], [**2ch WIDE** Wide]	(📖 76)
[Audio Limiter]	[**ON** On], [**OFF** Off]	(📖 76)
[Audio Compressor]	[H High], [L **Low**], [**OFF** Off]	(📖 77)
[MIC Att.]	[**ON** On], [**OFF** Off]	(📖 77)
[MIC Low Cut]	[**ON** On], [**OFF** Off]	(📖 77)
[MIC ALC Link]	[**LINK** **Linked**], [**SEP** Separated]	(📖 74)
[„S" Mic Att.]	[**ON** On], [**OFF** Off]	(📖 77)
[Headphone Volume]	Volume adjustment bar: 0 to 15 **(8)**, [🎧⟩] (softer), [🎧⟩⟩] (louder)	(📖 78)
[Speaker Volume]	Volume adjustment bar: 0 to 15 **(8)**, [◀] (softer), [◀⟩⟩] (louder)	
	In 〔MEDIA〕 mode only, this setting is an alternative way to adjust the built-in speaker's volume (📖 92).	
[Notification Sounds]	[▶■■⟩ **High Volume**], [▶■⟩ Low Volume], [**OFF** Off]	
	A beep will accompany some of the camcorder's operations. • While pre-recording is activated, the camcorder will not emit any notification sounds.	

[🗹 Display Setup] menu

Menu item	Setting options and additional information	
[Output Terminal]	[**OFF** Off], [**HDMI** HDMI]	(🔲 100)
[HDMI Max Resolution]	[3840x2160], [**1920x1080**], [1280x720]	(🔲 100)
[Output Status]	—	
	Displays a screen where you can check the configuration (video and audio) of the output signal.	
[LCD Brightness]	Brightness adjustment bar, [☀] (darker), [☀] (brighter)	
	• Changing the brightness of the screen does not affect the brightness of your recordings or the brightness of the playback image on a TV.	
[LCD Backlight]	[▪▪▪ Bright], [▪▪□ **Normal**], [▪□□ Dim]	
[Viewfinder Backlight]	[▪▪▪ Bright], [▪▪□ **Normal**]	
	Changes the screen's backlight level to one of three levels (LCD screen) or two levels (viewfinder), affecting the general brightness of the screen.	
	• Changing the brightness of the screen does not affect the brightness of your recordings or the brightness of the playback image on a TV.	
	• [▪▪▪ Bright] is not available for [LCD Backlight] while using a video light attached to the mini advanced shoe.	
[LCD Mirror Image]	[**ON** On], [**OFF** Off]	
	When this setting is set to [**ON** On], this function reverses the image on the screen horizontally when you rotate the LCD panel 180 degrees toward the subject. In other words, the screen will show a mirror image of the subject.	
[Output Onscreen Displays]	[**ON** On], [**OFF** Off]	
	When this setting is set to [**ON** On], the camcorder's onscreen displays will appear also on the screen of a TV or monitor connected to the camcorder.	
[Onscreen Markers]	[**OFF** Off], [▦G Level (Gray)], [▦W Level (White)], [▦G Grid (Gray)], [▦W Grid (White)]	
	You can display a grid or a horizontal line at the center of the screen. Use the markers as a reference to make sure your subject is framed correctly (vertically and/or horizontally).	
	• Using the onscreen markers will not affect the recordings.	
[Distance Units]	[**m** meters], [**ft** feet]	
	Selects the units to use for the focusing distance display while focusing manually. This setting also affects units for the altitude in the GPS information of geotagged recordings.	

[🔧 System Setup] menu

Menu item	Setting options and additional information	
[Language 🗊]	[Česky], [Dansk], [Deutsch], [Ελληνικά], [**English**], [Español], [Français], [Italiano], [Magyar], [Melayu], [Nederlands], [Norsk], [Polski], [Português], [Română], [Suomi], [Svenska], [Türkçe], [Русский], [Українська], [العربية], [فارسی], [ภาษาไทย], [简体中文], [繁體中文], [한국어], [日本語]	(🔲 28)
[Time Zone/DST]	[🏠] (home time zone), [✈] (travel time zone); For each: list of world time zones ([**New York**]), [☀] (DST adjustment): turn on or off **(off)**	(🔲 28)
[Date/Time]	Date and time adjustment fields; [Date Format]: [Y.M.D], [**M.D,Y**], [D.M.Y]; [24H]: turn on (24-hour clock) or off (12-hour clock) **(off)**	(🔲 27)
	In [Date Format] options, Y=year, M=month, D=day.	

126

Menu item	Setting options and additional information	
[Network Settings]		
[Connection Settings]	[1:] to [4:]	(□ 110)
	Default settings for profile [1: CameraAP]: [SSID]: **[GX10-xxxx-xx_Canon0C]**, [Password]: **[12345678]**	
	You can save up to 4 network configuration profiles in the camcorder. Initially, basic settings for a Camera Access Point connection are saved under network configuration profile [1: CameraAP].	
[Activate]	[Browser Remote], [Off]	(□ 112)
[Browser Remote Settings]		(□ 111)
[Port No.]	1 to 65535 (**[80]**)	
[Camcorder ID]	Camcorder identifier up to 8 characters (**[GX10]**)	
[FTP Transfer Settings]		(□ 119)
[FTP Server]	Server name up to 32 characters	
[FTP: User Name]	User name up to 32 characters	
[FTP: Password]	Password up to 32 characters	
[Destination Folder]	Destination folder's path up to 152 characters (Default is the root folder **[/]**)	
[Port No.]	1 to 65535 (**[21]**)	
[Passive Mode]	[On], **[Off]**	
[New Folder by Date]	**[On]**, [Off]	
[Same Named Files]	**[Skip]**, [Overwrite]	
[View Information]		(□ 112, 119)
[Fan]	[**A** Automatic], [**ON** On]	(□ 38)
[Wireless Remote Control]	[**ON** On], [**OFF** Off]	
	Allows the camcorder to be operated with the wireless controller.	
[POWER LED], [ACCESS LED]	[**ON** On], [**OFF** Off]	
	These settings determine whether the following LEDs and indicators will illuminate. [POWER LED]: The green POWER/CHG indicator (only when it serves as power indicator). [ACCESS LED]: The ACCESS indicator when the camcorder is accessing an SD card.	
[Auto Power Off]	[**ON** On], [**OFF** Off]	
	In order to save power when the camcorder is powered by a battery pack, when this setting is set to [**ON** On], the camcorder will automatically shut off if left without any operation for 5 minutes. • Approximately 30 seconds before the camcorder shuts off, [Auto Power Off] will appear.	
[REMOTE Terminal]	**RC-V100** RC-V100 (REMOTE A)], **Std.** Standard]	(□ 81)
[Assignable Button 1] to [Assignable Button 5]	Following are the default settings for each assignable button. For a complete list of the functions that can be assigned, refer to the detailed table. 1: [**AF/MF** AF/MF], 2: [**Powered IS**], 3: [**Pre REC**], 4: [**REC REVIEW** Rec Review], 5: [**MAGN.** Magnification]	(□ 86)
[Onscreen Assignable Button]	For a complete list of the functions that can be assigned, refer to the detailed table (default: [**PHOTO** Photo]).	(□ 86)
[CUSTOM Dial & Button]	[**Tv/Av/M** Tv/Av/M], [**GAIN** AGC Limit], [**Z** Exposure Comp.], [**OFF** Off]	(□ 85)
[Battery Info]	—	
	When you are using a battery pack that is compatible with Intelligent System, this option displays a screen where you can verify the battery charge (as a percentage) and the remaining recording time (**CAMERA** mode) or playback time (**MEDIA** mode). • If the battery pack is exhausted, the battery information may not be displayed.	
[Backup Menu Settings **B**]	[Save], [Load]	(□ 88)
[GPS Auto Time Setting]*	[**ON** Auto Update], [**OFF** Disable]	(□ 82)

Menu item	Setting options and additional information
[GPS Information Display]*	—
	When the optional GP-E2 GPS Receiver is attached to the camcorder, the following settings become available:
	[GPS Auto Time Setting]: You can have the camcorder automatically set the time based on the information acquired from GPS. For more details, refer to *Setting Time from GPS on the Camera* in the receiver's instruction manual.
	[GPS Information Display]: Displays the current GPS information. For more details, refer to *Viewing GPS Information* in the receiver's instruction manual.
[Certification Logo Display]	—
	Displays certification logos that apply to this camcorder.
	• This option may not be available depending on the country/region of purchase.
[Demo Mode]	[**ON** On], [**OFF** Off]
	The demonstration mode displays the camcorder's main features. It starts automatically when the camcorder is powered with the AC adapter if you leave it turned on without SD cards inserted for more than 5 minutes.
	• To cancel the demo mode once it has started, press any button or turn off the camcorder.
[Firmware]	—
	Displays the current firmware version of the camcorder.
	• This option is usually unavailable.
[Reset All]	[No], [Yes]
	Resets all the camcorder's settings to default values/settings.

* Option available only when the optional GP-E2 GPS Receiver is attached to the camcorder.

Troubleshooting

If you have a problem with your camcorder, refer to this section. Consult a Canon Service Center if the problem persists.

Power Source

The camcorder will not turn on or it turns off by itself.
- The battery pack is exhausted. Replace or charge the battery pack.
- Remove the battery pack and reattach it correctly.

Cannot charge the battery pack.
- Make sure the camcorder is off so charging can start.
- The temperature of the battery pack is outside the charging range (approximately 0 – 40 °C (32 – 104 °F)). Remove the battery pack, warm it or let it cool down, as necessary, and try charging it again.
- Charge the battery pack in temperatures between approximately 0 °C and 40 °C (32 °F and 104 °F).
- The battery pack is faulty. Replace the battery pack.
- The camcorder cannot communicate with the battery pack attached. Battery packs not recommended by Canon for use with this camcorder cannot be charged using this camcorder.
- If you are using a battery pack recommended by Canon for use with this camcorder, there may be a problem with the camcorder or battery pack. Consult a Canon Service Center.

A noise can be heard from the AC adapter.
- A faint sound can be heard while the AC adapter is connected to a power outlet. This is not a malfunction.

The battery pack is exhausted extremely quickly even at normal temperatures.
- The battery may have reached the end of its battery life. Buy a new battery pack.

Recording

Pressing the REC button will not start recording.
- You cannot record while the camcorder is writing previous recordings to an SD card (while the ACCESS indicator is illuminated in red). Wait until the camcorder has finished.
- The SD card is full. Delete some recordings (□ 93) or initialize the card (□ 31) to free some space.
- The file numbers have reached their maximum value. Insert a new SD card into the camcorder and set [🗗 Recording Setup] ❯ [File Numbering] to [Reset].

The point where the REC button was pressed does not match the beginning/end of the recording.
- There may be a slight interval between pressing the REC button and the actual start/end of recording. This is not a malfunction.

The camcorder will not focus.
- The camcorder may not be able to focus on certain subjects using autofocus. Focus manually (□ 45).
- When the AF mode is set to AF-boosted MF, start focusing manually until the AF frame changes to white (automatic adjustment range).
- The viewfinder is not adjusted. Use the dioptric adjustment lever to make the proper adjustment (□ 21).
- The lens is dirty. Clean the lens with a soft lens-cleaning cloth.

When a subject flits across in front of the lens, the image appears slightly bent.
- This is a phenomenon typical of CMOS image sensors. When a subject crosses very quickly in front of the camcorder, the image may seem slightly warped. This is not a malfunction.

Changing the operating mode between recording (●)/record standby (■)/playback (▶) takes longer than usual.
- When the SD card contains a large number of clips, some operations may take longer than usual. Save your recordings (□ 101) and initialize the card (□ 31). Alternatively, replace the SD card.

Clips or photos cannot be recorded properly.
- This may occur as clips and photos are recorded/deleted over time. Save your recordings (□ 101) and initialize the card (□ 31).

After using the camcorder for a long time, it becomes hot.
- The camcorder may become hot after using it continuously for long periods of time; this is not a malfunction. If the camcorder becomes unusually hot or it becomes hot after using it only for a short while, it may indicate a problem with the camcorder. Consult a Canon Service Center.

Playback

Cannot delete clips/photos
- The LOCK switch on the SD card is set to prevent accidental erasure. Change the position of the LOCK switch.
- Photos that were protected using other devices cannot be deleted with this camcorder.

Deleting clips takes longer than usual.
- When the SD card contains a large number of clips, some operations may take longer than usual. Save your recordings (□ 101) and initialize the card (□ 31).

Cannot copy clips/photos
- You may not be able to copy clips/photos recorded or edited using another device and then transferred to an SD card connected to the computer.

Cannot mark individual clips/photos in the index screen with a checkmark ✓
- You cannot select more than 100 clips/photos individually. Select the [All Clips] or [All Photos] option instead of [Select].

Indicators and Onscreen Displays

⟨■⟩ appears in red on the screen.
- Battery pack is exhausted. Replace or charge the battery pack.

⟨⟩ appears on the screen.
- The camcorder cannot communicate with the battery pack attached so the remaining battery time cannot be displayed.

Ⓐ/Ⓑ appears in red on the screen.
- The SD card is full. Delete some recordings (□ 93) to free some space or replace the card.

Ⓐⓢ/Ⓑⓢ appears in red on the screen.
- A card error occurred. Turn off the camcorder. Remove and reinsert the SD card. Initialize the SD card if the display does not change back to normal.

Even after stopping recording, the ACCESS indicator stays illuminated in red.
- The clip is being recorded on the card. This is not a malfunction.

The red POWER/CHG indicator flashes rapidly (one flash at 0.5-second intervals).
- The temperature of the battery pack is outside the charging range (approximately 0 – 40 °C (32 – 104 °F)). Remove the battery pack, warm it or let it cool down, as necessary, and try charging it again.
- Charge the battery pack in temperatures between approximately 0 °C and 40 °C (32 °F and 104 °F).
- The battery pack is damaged. Use a different battery pack.
- Charging has stopped because the AC adapter or the battery pack is faulty. Consult a Canon Service Center.

•⟨ flashes on the screen.
- You connected the optional GP-E2 GPS Receiver to the camcorder in MEDIA mode. Disconnect the receiver and connect it again after setting the camcorder to CAMERA mode.

⟨⟩ appears in yellow on the screen.
- The camcorder's internal temperature has reached a predetermined level. You can continue using the camcorder.

⟨⟩ appears in red on the screen.
- The camcorder's internal temperature has risen further while ⟨⟩ appeared in yellow on the screen. You can continue using the camcorder.

Picture and Sound

The screen appears too dark.
- Set [🖵 Display Setup] ❯ [LCD Backlight] to [Normal] or [Bright].

131

Screen displays turn on and off repeatedly.
- The battery pack is exhausted. Replace or charge the battery pack.
- Remove the battery pack and reattach it correctly.

Abnormal characters appear on the screen and the camcorder does not operate properly.
- Disconnect the power source and reconnect it after a short time.

Video noise appears on screen.
- Keep a distance between the camcorder and devices that emit strong electromagnetic fields (plasma TVs, cellular phones, etc.).

Horizontal bands appear on the screen.
- This is a phenomenon typical of CMOS image sensors when recording under some types of fluorescent, mercury or sodium lamps. This is not a malfunction. You may be able to reduce the symptoms by setting the shutter speed to a value matching the frequency of the local electrical system (1/100 for 50 Hz systems, 1/60 for 60 Hz systems).

Viewfinder picture is blurred.
- Adjust the viewfinder with the dioptric adjustment lever (□ 21).

No picture appears on the viewfinder.
- Pull out the viewfinder to activate it.

Audio cannot be recorded.
- The external microphone connected to the MIC terminal is not turned on or its battery is exhausted.
- The audio recording level is not set correctly (□ 74).

Sound is distorted or is recorded at lower levels.
- When recording near loud sounds (such as fireworks, shows or concerts), sound may become distorted or it may not be recorded at the actual levels. Activate the microphone attenuator (□ 74), or adjust the audio recording level manually.

The picture is displayed correctly but there is no sound from the built-in speaker.
- Speaker volume is turned off. Adjust the volume (□ 92).

SD Card and Accessories

Cannot insert the SD card.
- The SD card you are trying to insert is not facing the correct direction. Turn it over and insert it.

Cannot record on the SD card.
- The SD card is full. Delete some recordings (□ 93) to free some space or replace the SD card.
- Initialize the SD card using the [Complete Initialization] option (□ 31) when you use it with the camcorder for the first time.
- The LOCK switch on the SD card is set to prevent accidental erasure. Change the position of the LOCK switch.
- A compatible SD card must be used (□ 29).
- The folder and file numbers have reached their maximum value. Set [📷 Recording Setup] ❯ [File Numbering] to [Reset] and insert a new SD card.

The supplied wireless controller will not work.
- Set [✱ System Setup] ❯ [Wireless Remote Control] to [On].
- Replace the battery of the wireless controller.

The optional RC-V100 Remote Controller or commercially available remote control does not work.
- Make sure that [✱ System Setup] ❯ [REMOTE Terminal] is set to [RC-V100 (REMOTE A)] when using the optional RC-V100 Remote Controller or to [Standard] when using a commercially available remote control.
- Turn off the camcorder, reconnect the remote controller and then turn the camcorder back on again.

Connections with External Devices

Video noise appears on a nearby TV screen.
- When using the camcorder in a room where a TV is located, keep a distance between the AC adapter and the power or antenna cables of the TV.

Playback looks fine on the camcorder but there is no image on the external monitor.
- The camcorder is not connected correctly to the external monitor. Make sure you are using the correct connection (□ 99).
- The video input on the external monitor is not set to the video terminal to which you connected the camcorder. Select the correct video input.

The camcorder is connected using the supplied High Speed HDMI cable, but there is no picture or sound from the TV.
- Disconnect the High Speed HDMI cable and then restore the connection or turn the camcorder off and then on again.

The computer does not recognize the camcorder even though the camcorder is connected correctly.
- Disconnect the USB cable and turn off the camcorder. After a short while, turn it on again and restore the connection.
- Connect the camcorder to a different USB port on the computer.

Cannot transfer clips and photos to the computer.
- The SD card contains too many clips and photos. Delete some recordings until the SD card contains a combined total of 2,500 (Windows)/1,000 (macOS) or fewer recordings.

Network Functions

Check This First

> - Are the access point (wireless router), camcorder, computer or other network devices all turned on?
> - Is the network working and correctly configured?
> - Are all network devices correctly connected to the same network as the camcorder?
> - Are there any obstructions between the camcorder and the access point or between the network device used and the access point?

Cannot connect with an access point.
- There are other devices in the vicinity interfering with the wireless signal. Refer to *Precautions Regarding Wi-Fi Networks* (□ 133).
- Password information is not saved with the camcorder settings. When you load onto the camcorder settings from an SD card, all the passwords in the network-related settings are reset. Set up the network-related settings as necessary (□ 104).

Cannot establish a Camera Access Point connection with a network device.
- There are other devices in the vicinity interfering with the wireless signal. Refer to *Precautions Regarding Wi-Fi Networks* (□ 133).
- When you reset all the camcorder's settings, all network settings are lost as well. Set up the Camera Access Point settings again (□ 105).

The Browser Remote application will not start on the Web browser.
- Make sure Browser Remote is activated (□ 112).
- The URL entered into the Web browser's address bar is incorrect. Be sure to use the URL exactly as it appears in the information screen (□ 112).

The Browser Remote screen is not displayed correctly on the Web browser.
- The device, operating system or Web browser used may not be supported. For the latest information about supported systems, visit your local Canon Web site.
- Enable JavaScript and cookies in your Web browser's settings. For details, refer to the help modules or online documentation of the Web browser used.
- Delete the cache and cookies for Browser Remote's URL in your Web browser and restart Browser Remote.

Precautions Regarding Wi-Fi Networks

When using a Wi-Fi network, try the following corrective actions if the transmission rate drops, the connection is lost, or other problems occur.

Location of the access point (wireless router)
- When using a Wi-Fi network indoors, place the access point in the same room where you are using the camcorder.
- Place the access point in an open, unobstructed location, where people or objects do not come between it and the camcorder.
- Place the access point as close as possible to the camcorder.

Nearby electronic devices
- If the transmission rate over a Wi-Fi network drops because of interference from the following electronic devices, switching to the 5 GHz band or to a different channel may solve the problem.
- Wi-Fi networks using the IEEE 802.11b/g/n protocol operate in the 2.4 GHz band. For this reason, the transmission rate may drop if there are nearby microwave ovens, cordless telephones, microphones, or similar devices operating on the same frequency band.
- If another access point operating on the same frequency band as the camcorder is used nearby, the transmission rate may drop.

Using multiple camcorders/wireless transmitters/access points
- Check that there are no IP address conflicts among the devices connected to the same network.
- If multiple camcorders are connected to a single access point, connection speeds may be reduced.
- To reduce radio wave interference when there are multiple access points using IEEE 802.11b/g or IEEE 802.11n (in the 2.4 GHz band), leave a gap of four channels between each wireless access point. For example, use channels 1, 6, and 11, channels 2, 7, and 12, or channels 3, 8, and 13. If you can use IEEE 802.11a/n (in the 5 GHz band), switch to IEEE 802.11a/n and specify a different channel.

List of Messages

Refer to this section if a message appears on the screen. The messages in this section appear in alphabetical order. Note that for some messages, an indication of the SD card involved (Ⓐ, Ⓑ, etc.) may appear above the message itself.

For error messages related to network connections, refer to *Network Functions* (📖 135).

Accessing the memory card.   Do not remove the memory card.
- You opened the SD card compartment cover while the camcorder was accessing the SD card or the camcorder started accessing the card as you opened the SD card compartment cover. Do not remove the SD card until this message disappears.

Back up recordings regularly
- This message may appear when you turn on the camcorder. In the event of a malfunction, recordings may be lost so back up your recordings regularly.

Battery communication error.   Does this battery display the Canon logo?
- You attached a battery pack that is not recommended by Canon for use with this camcorder.
- If you are using a battery pack recommended by Canon for use with this camcorder, there may be a problem with the camcorder or battery pack. Consult a Canon Service Center.

Battery pack is not compatible. Turning off the camcorder.
- A battery pack not recommended by Canon for use with this camcorder was attached and the camcorder was turned on. The camcorder will automatically turn off in 4 seconds.

Cannot play back
- Clips cannot be played back from a 512 MB or smaller SD card. Use a compatible SD card (📖 29).

Cannot play back   Check the memory card
- There is a problem with the SD card. Save your recordings (📖 101) and initialize the card using the [Complete Initialization] option (📖 31). If the problem persists, use a different SD card.

Cannot play back   Initialize only using the camcorder
- The SD card in the camcorder was initialized using a computer. Initialize the card with this camcorder (📖 31).

Cannot record on this memory card
- Clips cannot be recorded on a 512 MB or smaller SD card. Use a compatible SD card (📖 29).

Cannot trim the scene
- Clips that were recorded or copied using other devices cannot be trimmed.

Charge the battery pack
- Battery pack is exhausted. Charge the battery pack.

Check the memory card
- Cannot access the SD card. Check the card and make sure it is inserted correctly.
- An SD card error occurred. The camcorder cannot record or display the image. Try removing and reinserting the card, or use a different SD card.
- You inserted a MultiMedia Card (MMC) into the camcorder. Use a compatible SD card (□ 29).
- If after the message disappears, A/B appears in red, perform the following: Turn off the camcorder and remove and reinsert the SD card. If A/B turns back to green you can resume recording/playback. If the problem persists, save your recordings (□ 101) and initialize the card (□ 31).

Fan error
- The cooling fan may not be working properly. Consult a Canon Service Center.

File name error
- The folder and file numbers have reached their maximum value. Set [✿ Recording Setup] ❯ [File Numbering] to [Reset] and delete all the clips and photos (□ 93) on the SD card or initialize it (□ 31).

Initialize only using the camcorder
- Initialize the SD card with this camcorder (□ 31).

May not be possible to record movies on this memory card
- You may not be able to record movies on an SD card without a Speed Class rating or rated SD Speed Class 2 or 4. Replace the SD card with one rated SD Speed Class 6 or 10, or UHS Speed Class U1 or U3.
- To record 4K clips with a resolution of [3840x2160 (150 Mbps)] and to use slow & fast motion recording, use SD cards rated UHS Speed Class U3.

Memory card cover is open
- After inserting an SD card, close the SD card compartment cover.

Memory card is full
- The SD card is full. Delete some recordings (□ 93) to free some space or replace the card.

Memory card is write-protected
- The LOCK switch on the SD card is set to prevent accidental erasure. Change the position of the LOCK switch.

No clips
- There are no clips on the SD card selected.

No memory card
- Insert a compatible SD card into the camcorder (□ 30).

No photos
- There are no photos to play back.

Operation canceled
- Clips cannot be recorded because the control data is corrupted or an encoder error has occurred. (Control data cannot be recovered with the camcorder.) Turn the camcorder off and the on again. Remove the SD cards and reinsert them, or replace them with new SD cards. If the problem persists, consult a Canon Service Center.

Process terminated with error
- The SD card compartment cover was opened during the complete initialization of an SD card or an error occurred during the initialization of an SD card. Initialize the card again. If the SD card still causes an error message, try replacing the SD card.

Recording was stopped due to insufficient write speed of the memory card
- The write speed of the SD card was too slow so recording was stopped. Replace the SD card with one rated SD Speed Class 6 or 10, or UHS Speed Class U1 or U3.
- To record 4K clips with a resolution of [3840x2160 (150 Mbps)] and to use slow & fast motion recording, use SD cards rated UHS Speed Class U3.
- After repeatedly recording, deleting and editing clips (fragmented memory), it will take longer to write data on the SD card and recording may stop. Save your recordings (□ 101) and initialize the card (□ 31).

Some clips could not be deleted
- Clips that were protected/edited with other devices and then transferred to an SD card connected to the computer cannot be deleted with this camcorder.

Task in progress. Do not disconnect the power source.
- The camcorder is updating the SD card. Wait until the operation ends and do not disconnect the AC adapter or remove the battery pack.

This photo cannot be displayed
- You may not be able to display photos taken with other devices or image files created or edited on a computer and then transferred to an SD card connected to the computer.

Too many photos and MP4 movies.   Disconnect the USB cable.
- The SD card contains too many MP4 clips and photos. Disconnect the USB cable and use a card reader to transfer the recordings from the SD card. Alternatively, delete MP4 clips and photos until the SD card contains a combined total of 2,500 (Windows)/1,000 (macOS) or fewer recordings and then connect the USB cable again.
- If a dialog box appeared on the computer screen, close it. Disconnect the USB cable, and restore the connection after a short while.

Unable to recognize the data
- The camcorder cannot recognize data that was recorded using a video configuration that is not supported (PAL or SECAM).

Unable to recover data
- Could not recover a corrupted file. Save your recordings (□ 101) and initialize the SD card using the [Complete Initialization] option (□ 31).
- The camcorder may not be able to recover clips when there is not enough space on the SD card. Delete some clips (□ 93) to free some space.

Network Functions

Along with this list, refer also to the instruction manuals of the access point or other external devices you are using.

A User is already accessing the server. Try again later.
- This message appears on the screen of the connected device. Another device connected to the network is already operating the camcorder. To use this device, first end the connection on the device accessing the camcorder and then touch Retry.

An error occurred during FTP communication.   File transfer was not completed.
- An error occurred while transferring files to the FTP server. Turn the camcorder and the FTP server off and then on again and try again the FTP transfer (□ 120).

Cannot log in to FTP server.
- Check the user name and password information in the FTP server settings (□ 119).

Cannot transfer files to FTP server.
- Check that there is enough available space in the data storage device (hard disk, etc.) that contains the destination folder on the FTP server.

IP address conflict
- Another device on the same network has the same IP address assigned to the camcorder. Change the IP address of the conflicting device or the camcorder.

Memory card cover is open
- The SD card compartment cover was opened while the SD card was being accessed. Stop the network function in use and end the network connection.

Multiple access points detected. Try the operation again.
- There are multiple access points sending out a WPS signal at the same time. Try the operation again later or perform setup using the [WPS: PIN Code] or [Search for Access Points] option (□ 108).

Network is not working correctly
- There's a hardware problem with the camcorder's network related circuitry. Try turning the camcorder off and the on again. If the problem persists, consult a Canon Service Center.

No access points found
- The camcorder searched for active Wi-Fi networks (access points) in the area but none were found. Make sure the access point is working correctly and try connecting again.
- The access point is operating in stealth mode. Deactivate the stealth function in the wireless router (access point) settings.
- The camcorder may not be able to find the access point if MAC address filtering is activated. Check the camcorder's MAC address with the [♥ System Setup] ❯ [Network Settings] ❯ [View Information] setting and add the camcorder's MAC address to the list of approved wireless devices in the wireless router (access point) settings.

Reached the end of the adjustment range
- This message appears on the screen of the connected device. While adjusting the focus remotely using Browser Remote, the lens reached the end of its available range.

Some files could not be transferred.
- The file system is corrupted or you attempted to transfer clips not recorded with this camcorder. Delete those clips from the SD card and then transfer the files again (□ 120).
- The destination folder contains files with the same file name as those to be transferred. Rename the files or set [♥ System Setup] ❯ [Network Settings] ❯ [FTP Transfer Settings] ❯ [Same Named Files] to [Overwrite] to overwrite the files in the destination folder.

Unable to complete WPS.

- Turn off the camcorder and access point. After a short while, turn them on again and try again. If the problem persists, perform setup using the [Search for Access Points] option (📖 108).

Unable to complete WPS. Try the operation again.

- More than 2 minutes passed between activating WPS on the access point and touching [OK] on the camcorder. Start over the WPS procedure from the beginning.
- The WPS button was not held down long enough. Refer to the instruction manual of your wireless router and make sure to keep the WPS button held down until the wireless router's WPS function is activated.
- The access point's encryption method is set to [WEP]. Wi-Fi Protected Setup (WPS) cannot connect to access points set to this encryption method. Change the access point's encryption method or use another connection method (📖 106).

Unable to connect

- Could not connect to the access point or network device selected.
- Cordless phones, microwave ovens, refrigerators and other appliances may interfere with the wireless signal. Try using the camcorder in a location farther away from such appliances.

Unable to connect to FTP server.

- Could not connect to the FTP server. Check the FTP server settings (📖 119).

Unable to obtain an IP address

- If you are not using a DHCP server, connect using the [Manual] option and enter the IP address using the [Manual] option (📖 104).
- Turn on the DHCP server. If it is already on, make sure it is functioning properly.
- Make sure the address range for the DHCP server is sufficient.
- If you are not using a DNS server, set the DNS address to [0.0.0.0].
- Set the DNS server's IP address in the camcorder.
- Turn on the DNS server. If it is already on, make sure it is functioning properly.
- Make sure that the DNS server's IP address and the name for that address are correctly configured.
- If you are using a wireless gateway router, make sure all of the devices in the network, including the camcorder, are configured with the correct gateway address.

Wi-Fi authentication unsuccessful

- Make sure the camcorder and access point are using the same authentication/encryption method and encryption key.
- If the access point is using MAC address filtering, check the camcorder's MAC address with the [✿ System Setup] ❯ [Network Settings] ❯ [View Information] setting and add the camcorder's MAC address to the list of approved wireless devices in the wireless router (access point) settings.

Wi-Fi connection terminated

- An error occurred on the access point or connected device. Check the network or connected device and try connecting again.
- The Wi-Fi signal became too weak and the wireless connection was lost. Wait a moment or turn off other devices in the area that may be interfering with the Wi-Fi signal and then try connecting again.

Wi-Fi error.   Incorrect authentication method.

- Make sure the camcorder and access point are using the same authentication/encryption method and encryption key.
- If the access point is using MAC address filtering, check the camcorder's MAC address with the [✿ System Setup] ❯ [Network Settings] ❯ [View Information] setting and add the camcorder's MAC address to the list of approved wireless devices in the wireless router (access point) settings.

Wi-Fi error.   Incorrect encryption key.

- When the authentication method was set to [WPA-PSK], [WPA2-PSK] or [Shared Key], or the encryption method was set to [WEP], the encryption key (WEP key or AES / TKIP password) entered or its length (number of characters) is incorrect. Valid password length varies depending on the encryption method:
  AES / TKIP encryption: 8 to 63 ASCII characters or 64 hexadecimal characters.
  64-bit WEP encryption: 5 ASCII characters or 10 hexadecimal characters.
  128-bit WEP encryption: 13 ASCII characters or 26 hexadecimal characters.

Wi-Fi error.   Incorrect encryption method.

- Make sure the camcorder and access point are using the same authentication/encryption method.
- If the access point is using MAC address filtering, check the camcorder's MAC address with the [✿ System Setup] ❯ [Network Settings] ❯ [View Information] setting and add the camcorder's MAC address to the list of approved wireless devices in the wireless router (access point) settings.

Safety Instructions and Handling Precautions

Be sure to read these instructions in order to operate the product safely. Follow these instructions to prevent injury or harm to the operator of the product or others.

⚠ WARNING
Denotes the risk of serious injury or death.

- Stop using the product in any case of unusual circumstances such as the presence of smoke or a strange smell.
- Do not touch any exposed internal parts.
- Do not get the product wet. Do not insert foreign objects or liquids into the product.
- Do not touch the product connected to a power outlet during lightning storms. This may cause electric shock.
- Do not disassemble or modify the product.
- Do not expose the product to strong shocks or vibration.
- Observe the following instructions when using commercially available batteries or provided battery packs.
  - Use batteries/battery packs only with their specified product.
  - Do not heat batteries/battery packs or expose them to fire.
  - Do not charge batteries/battery packs using non-authorized battery chargers.
  - Do not expose the terminals to dirt or let them come into contact with metallic pins or other metal objects.
  - Do not use leaking batteries/battery packs. If a battery/battery pack leaks and the material contacts your skin or clothing, flush the exposed area thoroughly with running water. In case of eye contact, flush thoroughly with copious amounts of clean running water and seek immediate medical assistance.
  - When disposing of batteries/battery packs, insulate the terminals with tape or other means. This may cause electric shock, explosion or fire.
- Use only power sources specified in this instruction manual for use with the product.
- Observe the following instructions when using a battery charger or AC adapter.
  - Do not plug in or unplug the product with wet hands.
  - Do not use the product if the power plug is not fully inserted into the power outlet.
  - Do not expose the power plug and terminals to dirt or let them come into contact with metallic pins or other metal objects.
  - Do not place heavy objects on the power cord. Do not damage, break or modify the power cord.
  - Do not wrap the product in cloth or other materials when in use or shortly after use when the product is still warm in temperature.
  - Do not unplug the product by pulling the power cord.
  - Do not leave the product connected to a power source for long periods of time.
- Do not allow the product to maintain contact with the same area of skin for extended periods of time during use. This may result in low-temperature contact burns, including skin redness and blistering, even if the product does not feel hot. The use of a tripod or similar equipment is recommended when using the product in hot places and for people with circulation problems or less sensitive skin.
- Keep the product out of the reach of young children.
- Periodically remove any dust buildup from the power plug and power outlet using a dry cloth.
- Follow any indications to turn off the product in places where its use is forbidden. Not doing so may cause other equipment to malfunction due to the effect of electromagnetic waves and even result in accidents.

⚠ CAUTION
Denotes the risk of injury.

- Do not leave the product in places exposed to extremely high or low temperatures. The product may become extremely hot/cold and cause burns or injury when touched.
- Only mount the product on a tripod that is sufficiently sturdy.
- Do not look at the screen or through the viewfinder for prolonged periods of time. This may induce symptoms similar to motion sickness. In such a case, stop using the product immediately and rest for a while before resuming use.

Camcorder

Be sure to observe the following precautions to ensure maximum performance.

- **Save your recordings periodically.** Make sure to transfer your recordings to a computer (□ 101) and save them on a regular basis. This will protect your important recordings in case of damage and create more free space on the SD card. Canon shall not be liable for any data loss.
- Do not use or store the camcorder in dusty or sandy places. The camcorder is not waterproof – avoid also water, mud or salt. If any of the above should get into the camcorder it may damage the camcorder and/or the lens.
- Do not use the camcorder near strong electromagnetic fields such as near powerful magnets and motors, MRI machines or high-voltage power lines. Using the camcorder in such places may cause anomalies in the video, or audio or video noise to appear.
- Do not point the camcorder or viewfinder toward an intense light source, such as the sun on a sunny day or an intense artificial light source. Doing so may damage the image sensor or the camcorder's internal components. Be careful especially when using a tripod or shoulder strap. When the camcorder is not in use, keep the lens barrier closed.
- Do not carry the camcorder by the LCD panel. Be careful when closing the LCD panel. When using a wrist strap, do not allow the camcorder to swing and hit an object.
- **Handle the touch screen with care.** Do not apply excessive force and do not use ballpoint pens or other hard-tipped tools to operate the touch screen. This may damage the touch screen's surface.
- Do not attach protective film on the touch screen. The camcorder features a capacitive touch screen so you may not be able to correctly operate the touch screen with an additional protective layer.
- When mounting the camcorder on a tripod, make sure that the tripod's fastening screw is shorter than 6 mm (0.24 in.). Using other tripods may damage the camcorder.

6 mm

- **When recording movies, try to get a calm, stable picture.** Excessive camcorder movement while shooting and extensive use of fast zooms and panning can result in jittery scenes. In extreme cases, the playback of such scenes may result in visually induced motion sickness. If you experience such a reaction, stop the playback immediately and take a rest break as necessary.

Long-term storage
If you do not intend to use the camcorder for a long time, store it in a place free of dust, in low humidity, and at temperatures not higher than 30 °C (86 °F).

Battery Pack

> **DANGER!**
> **Treat the battery pack with care.**
> - Keep it away from fire (or it might explode).
> - Do not expose the battery pack to temperature higher than 60 °C (140 °F). Do not leave it near a heater or inside a car in hot weather.
> - Do not try to disassemble or modify it.
> - Do not drop it or subject it to shocks.
> - Do not get it wet.

- Dirty terminals may cause a poor contact between the battery pack and the camcorder. Wipe the terminals with a soft cloth.

Long-term storage

- Store battery packs in a dry place at temperatures no higher than 30 °C (86 °F).
- To extend the battery life of the battery pack, discharge it completely before storing it.
- Charge and discharge all your battery packs fully at least once a year.

Remaining battery time

When you are using a battery pack that is compatible with Intelligent System, if the remaining battery time displayed is not correct, charge the battery pack fully. Still, the correct time may not be displayed if a fully charged battery pack is used continuously in high temperatures or it is left unused for long periods of time. Also, the correct remaining time may not be displayed, depending on the battery life. Use the time shown on the screen as an approximation.

SD Card

- We recommend backing up the recordings on the SD card onto your computer. Data may be corrupted or lost due to card defects or exposure to static electricity. Canon shall not be liable for lost or corrupted data.
- Do not touch or expose the terminals to dust or dirt.
- Do not use SD cards in places subject to strong magnetic fields.
- Do not leave SD cards in places subject to high humidity and high temperature.
- Do not disassemble, bend, drop, or subject SD cards to shocks and do not expose them to water.
- Check the direction before inserting the SD card. Forcing an SD card into a slot if it is not correctly oriented may damage the card or the camcorder.
- Do not attach any labels or stickers on the SD card.

Disposal

When you delete clips or initialize an SD card, only the file allocation table is altered and stored data is not physically erased. When you dispose of an SD card or give either to another person, initialize it using the [Complete Initialization] option (📖 31). Fill it up with unimportant recordings, and then initialize it again using the same option. This makes recovering the original recordings very difficult.

Built-in Rechargeable Lithium Battery

The camcorder has a built-in rechargeable lithium battery to keep the date/time and other settings. The built-in lithium battery is recharged while you use the camcorder; however, it will discharge completely if you do not use the camcorder for about 3 months.

To recharge the built-in lithium battery: Connect the AC adapter to the camcorder and leave it connected for 24 hours with the camcorder off.

Lithium Button Battery

WARNING!
- The battery used in this device may present a fire or chemical burn hazard if mishandled.
- Do not disassemble, modify, immerse in water, heat above 100 °C (212 °F) or incinerate the battery.
- Do not insert the battery into the mouth. If swallowed, seek medical assistance immediately. The battery case may break and the battery fluids may cause internal injuries.
- Keep the battery out of the reach of children.
- Do not recharge, short-circuit or insert the battery in the wrong direction.
- Dispose of the used battery according to applicable recycling regulations.

- Do not pick up the battery using tweezers or other metal tools, as this will cause a short circuit.
- Wipe the battery with a clean dry cloth to ensure proper contact.

Maintenance/Others

Cleaning

Camcorder body

- Use a soft, dry cloth to clean the camcorder's body. Never use chemically treated cloths or volatile solvents such as paint thinner.

Lens

- Remove any dust or dirt particles using a non-aerosol type blower.
- Use a clean, soft lens-cleaning cloth to gently wipe the lens. Never use tissue paper.

LCD screen

- Clean the LCD screen using a clean, soft lens-cleaning cloth and commercially available fluid for eyeglasses.
- Condensation may form on the surface of the screen when the temperature changes suddenly. Wipe it with a soft dry cloth.

Condensation

Moving the camcorder rapidly between hot and cold temperatures may cause condensation (water droplets) to form on its internal surfaces. Stop using the camcorder if condensation is detected. Continued use may damage the camcorder.

Condensation may form in the following cases:

- When the camcorder is moved quickly from cold to warm places
- When the camcorder is left in a humid room
- When a cold room is heated rapidly

To avoid condensation

- Do not expose the camcorder to sudden or extreme changes in temperature.
- Remove the SD cards and battery pack. Then, place the camcorder in an airtight plastic bag and let it adjust gradually to temperature changes before removing it from the bag.

When condensation is detected

The precise time required for water droplets to evaporate will vary depending on the location and weather conditions. As a general rule, wait for 2 hours before resuming use of the camcorder.

Optional Accessories (availability differs from area to area)

This product is designed to achieve excellent performance when used with **genuine Canon accessories**. Canon shall not be liable for any damage to this product and/or accidents such as fire, etc., caused by the malfunction of non-genuine Canon accessories (e.g., a leakage and/or explosion of a battery pack). Please note that this warranty does not apply to repairs arising out of the malfunction of non-genuine Canon accessories, although you may request such repairs on a chargeable basis.

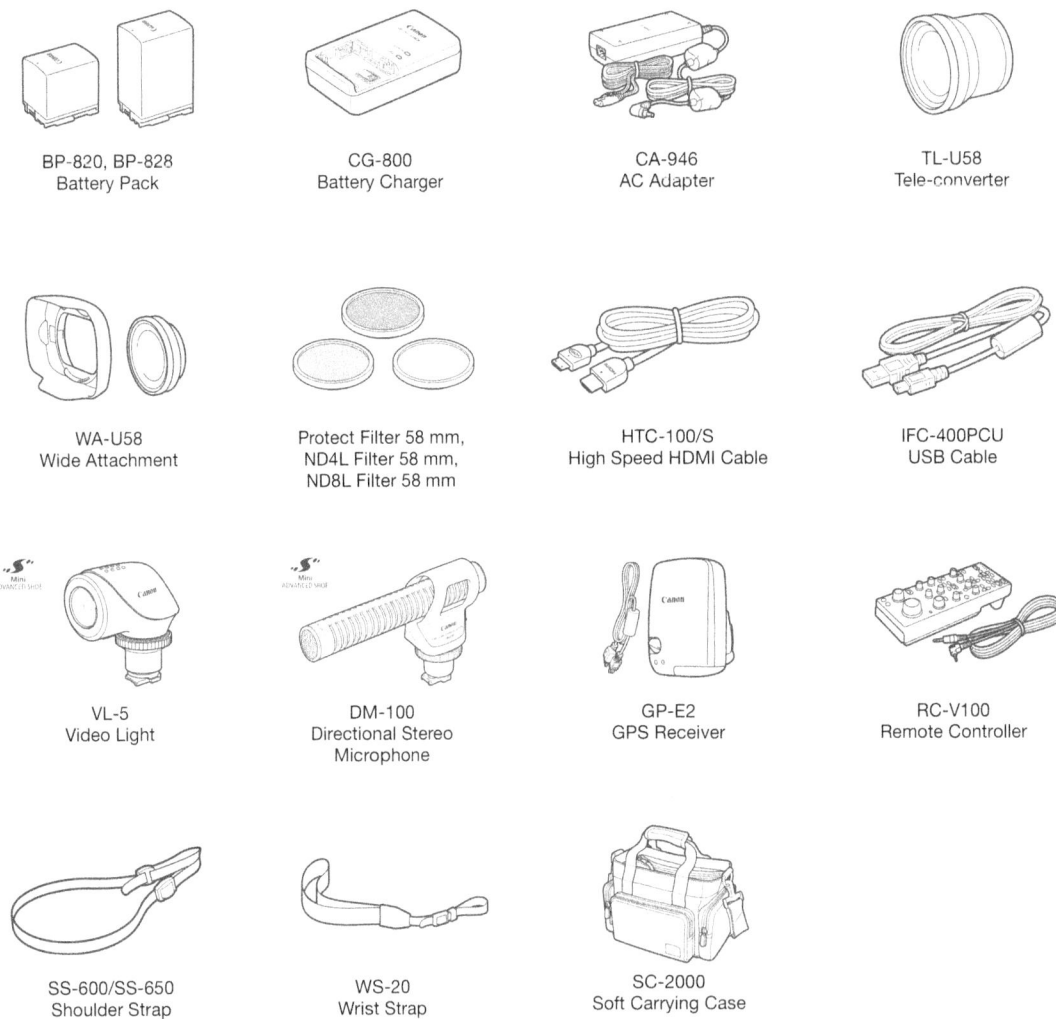

BP-820, BP-828
Battery Pack

CG-800
Battery Charger

CA-946
AC Adapter

TL-U58
Tele-converter

WA-U58
Wide Attachment

Protect Filter 58 mm,
ND4L Filter 58 mm,
ND8L Filter 58 mm

HTC-100/S
High Speed HDMI Cable

IFC-400PCU
USB Cable

VL-5
Video Light

DM-100
Directional Stereo
Microphone

GP-E2
GPS Receiver

RC-V100
Remote Controller

SS-600/SS-650
Shoulder Strap

WS-20
Wrist Strap

SC-2000
Soft Carrying Case

(i) NOTES

• Accessories that are compatible with the Advanced Accessory Shoe cannot be attached to this camcorder. Look for the **Mini ADVANCED SHOE** logo to ensure compatibility with the mini advanced shoe.

Call or visit your local retailer/dealer for genuine Canon video accessories. You can also obtain genuine accessories for your Canon camcorder by calling: 1-800-828-4040, Canon U.S.A. Information Center.

Battery Packs

When you need extra battery packs, select one of the following models: BP-820 or BP-828.

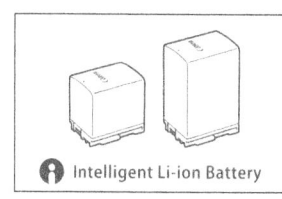

When you use battery packs bearing the Intelligent System mark, the camcorder will communicate with the battery and display the remaining usage time (accurate to 1 minute). You can only use and charge these battery packs with camcorders and chargers compatible with Intelligent System.

143

CG-800 Battery Charger

Use the battery charger to charge the battery packs. It plugs directly into a power outlet without a cable.

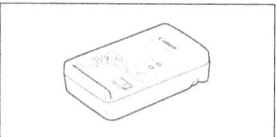

TL-U58 Tele-Converter

- The minimum focusing distance at full telephoto with the tele-converter is 1.3 m (4.3 ft.).
- The tele-converter cannot be used together with the supplied lens hood.

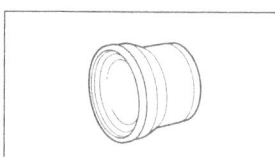

WA-U58 wide attachment

- The wide attachment cannot be used together with the supplied lens hood.

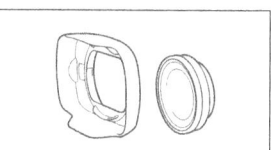

This mark identifies genuine Canon video accessories. When you use Canon video equipment, we recommend Canon-brand accessories or products bearing the same mark.

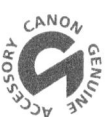

Specifications

VIXIA GX10

♦ — Values given are approximate figures.

System

- **Recording System**
  Movies:
    Video format: MPEG-4 AVC/H.264
    Audio format: MPEG-4 AAC-LC, 16 bit, 48 kHz, 2 channels
    File format: MP4
  Photos:
    DCF (Design rule for Camera File system), compatible with Exif Ver. 2.3[1], JPEG compression
    [1]This camcorder supports Exif 2.3 (also called "Exif Print"). Exif Print is a standard for enhancing the communication between camcorders and printers. By connecting to an Exif Print-compliant printer, the camcorder's image data at the time of shooting is used and optimized, yielding extremely high quality prints.

- **Video Configuration (recording/playback)**
  Bit rate: 150 Mbps, 35 Mbps, 17 Mbps, 8 Mbps, 4 Mbps
  Resolution: 3840x2160, 1920x1080, 1280x720
  Color sampling: 4:2:0, 8 bit
  Frame rate: 59.94P, 29.97P, 23.98P

- **Recording Media (not included)**
  For approximate recording times, refer to the *Reference Tables* (□ 147)
  SD, SDHC (SD High Capacity) or SDXC (SD eXtended Capacity) card (2 slots)

- **Image Sensor**
  1.0-inch single-plate CMOS sensor
  Effective pixels: 8,290,000 pixels♦ (3840x2160)

- **LCD Touch Screen**
  3.5 in. color LCD, 16:9 aspect ratio, 1,560,000 dots♦, 100% coverage, capacitive touch screen operation

- **Viewfinder:** 0.24 in., equivalent to 1,560,000 dots♦, 100% coverage

- **Microphone:** Stereo electret condenser microphone

- **Lens**
  f=8.3 – 124.5 mm, F/2.8 – 4.5, 15x optical zoom, 9-blade iris diaphragm
  35mm equivalent focal length: 25.5 – 382.5 mm♦

- **Lens Configuration**
  18 elements in 14 groups (2 aspheric elements)

- **Filter Diameter:** 58 mm

- **Focus**
  Manual focus, AF-boosted MF, continuous AF
  AF type: Dual Pixel CMOS AF, contrast-detection AF
  Minimum focusing distance: 60 cm (2 ft.); 1 cm (0.39 in.) at full wide angle

- **White Balance**
  Automatic white balance (AWB); 2 preset settings (daylight, tungsten lamp); color temperature setting; custom white balance (2 sets)

- **Minimum Illumination**♦
  0.1 lx (shooting mode [◒ Low Light], shutter speed 1/2)
  1.7 lx (59.94P, shooting mode [**P** Programmed AE], auto slow shutter [On], shutter speed 1/30)

- **Image Stabilization**
  Optical-shift image stabilizer + digital compensation (Standard IS, Dynamic IS, Powered IS)

- Size of Photos: 3840x2160, 1920x1080, 1280x720

Wi-Fi

- Wireless Standard: IEEE802.11b/g/n (2.4 GHz band), IEEE802.11a/n (5 GHz band)
- Connection Methods
  Infrastructure (Wi-Fi Protected Setup (WPS), search for access points, manual), Camera Access Point
- Authentication Methods: Open, shared key, WPA-PSK, WPA2-PSK
- Encryption Methods: WEP-64, WEP-128, TKIP, AES
- Available Wi-Fi Channels
  2.4 GHz band: CH1 to CH11
  5 GHz band: CH56 to CH64 (Infrastructure only), CH149 to CH161 (Infrastructure/Camera Access Point)

Terminals

- HDMI OUT Terminal: HDMI mini connector, output only
- USB Terminal: mini-B receptacle, Hi-Speed USB, output only
- MIC Terminal
  ∅ 3.5 mm stereo mini-jack (unbalanced)
  –65 dBV (auto volume, full scale –12 dB) / 5 kΩ or more
  Microphone attenuator: 20 dB
- ∩ (headphone) Terminal
  ∅ 3.5 mm stereo mini-jack (unbalanced)
  –29 dBV (16 Ω load, Max volume) / 100 Ω
- REMOTE Terminal: ∅ 2.5 mm stereo sub-mini jack, input only

Power/Others

- Power Supply (rated)
  7.4 V DC (battery pack), 8.4 V DC (AC adapter)
- Power Consumption♦
  (Recording video configuration: 3840x2160, 150 Mbps, 59.94P, autofocus activated, LCD/viewfinder backlight at [Normal])
  Using only the LCD screen: 8.5 W
  Using only the viewfinder: 7.9 W
- Operating Temperature♦: 0 – 40 °C (32 – 104 °F)
- Dimensions♦ [W x H x D] (excluding the grip belt)
  Camcorder only: 135 x 97 x 214 mm (5.3 x 3.8 x 8.4 in.)
  Camcorder with the lens hood attached: 150 x 97 x 267 mm (5.9 x 3.8 x 10.5 in.)
- Weight♦
  Camcorder body only (including the grip belt): 1,140 g (2.5 lb.)
  Typical recording configuration*: 1,355 g (3.0 lb.)
  * Camcorder with lens hood, BP-828 battery pack and one SD card.

CA-946 AC Adapter

- Rated Input: 100 – 240 V AC, 50/60 Hz
- Rated Output: 65 VA (100 V AC) - 85 VA (240 V AC)
- Operating Temperature[♦]: 0 – 40 °C (32 – 104 °F)
- Dimensions[♦]: 73 x 40 x 139 mm (2.9 x 1.6 x 5.5 in.)
- Weight[♦]: 465 g (1.0 lb.)

BP-828 Battery Pack

- Battery Type
  Rechargeable lithium ion battery, compatible with Intelligent System
- Nominal Voltage: 7.4 V DC
- Nominal Capacity: 2,670 mAh
- Rated Capacity (minimum): 19 Wh / 2,550 mAh
- Operating Temperature[♦]: 0 – 40 °C (32 – 104 °F)
- Dimensions[♦]: 30.7 x 55.7 x 40.2 mm (1.2 x 2.2 x 1.6 in.)
- Weight[♦]: 121 g (4.3 oz.)

Weight and dimensions are approximate. Errors and omissions excepted.

Reference Tables

Charging Times

Charging times are approximate and vary according to charging conditions and initial charge of the battery pack.

Battery pack→ Charging conditions↓	BP-820	BP-828
Using the camcorder and supplied CA-946 AC adpater	230 min.	350 min.
Using the CG-800 Battery Charger	190 min.	260 min.

Approximate Recording Time on an SD Card

Resolution	SD card capacity				
	8 GB	16 GB	32 GB	64 GB	128 GB
3840x2160 (150 Mbps)	5 min.	10 min.	25 min.	55 min.	1 h. 50 min.
1920x1080 (35 Mbps)	25 min.	55 min.	1 h. 55 min.	4 h.	8 h. 5 min.
1920x1080 (17 Mbps)	55 min.	2 h.	4 h. 5 min.	8 h. 15 min.	16 h. 35 min.
1280x720 (8 Mbps)	2 h.	4 h. 15 min.	8 h. 40 min.	17 h. 35 min.	35 h. 20 min.
1280x720 (4 Mbps)	4 h. 5 min.	8 h. 35 min.	17 h. 25 min.	35 h. 15 min.	70 h. 45 min.

Approximate Recording Times with a Fully Charged Battery Pack

The usage times in the following tables are approximate and were measured under the following conditions. Actual times may vary.
- Only the LCD screen was used.
- "Typical recording" times measure recording times with repeated operations such as start/stop recording, zooming and turning on/off the camcorder.

The effective usage time of the battery pack may decrease when using a bright screen setting, when recording in cold surroundings, etc.

Video configuration		Usage conditions	Battery pack	
Resolution (bit rate)	Frame rate		BP-820 (optional)	BP-828 (supplied)
3840x2160 (150 Mbps)	59.94P	Recording (maximum)	80 min.	120 min.
		Recording (typical)	40 min.	60 min.
		Playback	115 min.	175 min.
	29.97P	Recording (maximum)	100 min.	150 min.
		Recording (typical)	45 min.	70 min.
		Playback	135 min.	205 min.
1920x1080 (35 Mbps)	59.94P	Recording (maximum)	90 min.	145 min.
		Recording (typical)	45 min.	70 min.
		Playback	145 min.	220 min.
	29.97P	Recording (maximum)	110 min.	165 min.
		Recording (typical)	50 min.	80 min.
		Playback	150 min.	230 min.

| Video configuration | | Usage conditions | Battery pack | |
Resolution (bit rate)	Frame rate		BP-820 (optional)	BP-828 (supplied)
1280x720 (8 Mbps)	59.94P	Recording (maximum)	95 min.	140 min.
		Recording (typical)	45 min.	70 min.
		Playback	150 min.	230 min.
1280x720 (4 Mbps)	29.97P	Recording (maximum)	115 min.	170 min.
		Recording (typical)	55 min.	80 min.
		Playback	155 min.	235 min.

Index

CANON CONSUMER DIGITAL VIDEO EQUIPMENT LIMITED WARRANTY FOR THE UNITED STATES

The limited warranty set forth below is given by Canon U.S.A., Inc. ("Canon USA") with respect to Canon Consumer Digital Video Equipment (the "Equipment") purchased in the United States. This limited warranty is only effective upon presentation of your Bill of Sale or other proof of purchase. The Equipment is warranted under normal, non-commercial, personal use, against defective materials or workmanship as follows:

Parts: Defective parts will be exchanged for new parts or comparable rebuilt parts for a period of ONE YEAR from the date of original purchase, except for a defective Video Head, which will be exchanged for a period of three months from the date of purchase.

Labor: For a period of ONE YEAR from the date of original purchase, labor will be provided free of charge by our factory service centers or designated service facilities located in the United States.

When returning Equipment under this warranty, you must pre-pay the shipping charges, and you must enclose the Bill of Sale or other proof of purchase with a complete explanation of the problem. During the ONE-YEAR warranty period, repairs will be made and the Equipment will be return-shipped to you free of charge. For repairs after the warranty period is over, you will be given an estimate of the cost of repair and an opportunity to approve or disapprove of the repair expense before it is incurred. If you approve, repairs will be made and the Equipment will be return-shipped to you. (shipping charges apply). If you disapprove, we will return-ship the equipment at no charge to you.

Non-Canon brand peripheral equipment and software which may be distributed with, or factory loaded on, the Equipment, are sold "AS IS" without warranty of any kind by Canon USA, including any implied warranty regarding merchantability or fitness for a particular purpose. The sole warranty with respect to such non-Canon brand items is given by the manufacturer or producer thereof. If the Equipment contains a hard disk drive, Canon USA recommends that data stored on that drive be duplicated or backed up to prevent its loss in the event of failure or other malfunction of such drive.

Canon USA shall have no responsibility under this limited warranty for use of the Equipment in conjunction with incompatible peripheral equipment and incompatible software.

In order to obtain warranty service, contact the authorized Canon retail dealer from whom you purchased the Equipment or call the CANON INFORMATION CENTER AT 1-800-OK-CANON). You will be directed to the nearest service facility for your Equipment.

This Limited Warranty covers all defects encountered in normal use of the Equipment and does not apply in the following cases:

    A) Loss or damage to the Equipment due to abuse, mishandling, accident, improper maintenance, or failure to follow operating instructions;

    B) If the Equipment is defective as a result of leaking batteries, sand, dirt or water damage;

    C) If defects or damages are caused by the use of unauthorized parts or by service other than by Canon USA's factory service centers or authorized service facilities;

    D) If the Equipment is used for commercial or industrial use.

This Limited Warranty does not cover cabinet (exterior finish), video cassette tape, head cleanings, nor does it apply to Equipment purchased outside the United States. This warranty does not cover units sold to rental firms, military operations, hotels, schools, hospitals or for other commercial, industrial, or institutional applications. These uses are covered only by such specific warranty as Canon may issue with such sales.

This Limited Warranty does not apply to accessories or consumables for the Equipment, which are sold "AS IS", without warranty of any kind by Canon USA.

Please retain this warranty card and your Bill of Sale as a permanent record of your purchase. This card is most important in order to be sure you are contacted right away should there be a safety inspection, modification or product recall under applicable laws or regulations.

NO IMPLIED WARRANTY, INCLUDING MERCHANTABILITY AND FITNESS FOR A PARTICULAR PURPOSE APPLIES TO THIS EQUIPMENT AFTER THE APPLICABLE PERIOD OF EXPRESS WARRANTY OR GUARANTY, EXCEPT AS MENTIONED ABOVE, GIVEN BY ANY PERSON, FIRM OR CORPORATION WITH RESPECT TO THIS EQUIPMENT SHALL BIND THE UNDERSIGNED (SOME STATES DO NOT ALLOW LIMITATIONS ON HOW LONG AN IMPLIED WARRANTY LASTS, SO THE ABOVE LIMITATION OR EXCLUSION MAY NOT APPLY TO YOU). CANON USA SHALL NOT BE LIABLE FOR LOSS OF REVENUES OR PROFITS, EXPENSE FOR SUBSTITUTE EQUIPMENT OR SERVICE, STORAGE CHARGES, LOSS OR CORRUPTION OF DATA, INCLUDING WITHOUT LIMITATION, LOSS OR CORRUPTION OF DATA STORED ON THE EQUIPMENT'S HARD DRIVE, OR ANY OTHER SPECIAL, INCIDENTAL OR CONSEQUENTIAL DAMAGES CAUSED BY THE USE, MISUSE OR INABILITY TO USE THE EQUIPMENT, REGARDLESS OF THE LEGAL THEORY ON WHICH THE CLAIM IS BASED, AND EVEN IF CANON USA HAS BEEN ADVISED OF THE POSSIBILITY OF SUCH DAMAGES. NOR SHALL RECOVERY OF ANY KIND AGAINST CANON USA BE GREATER THAN THE PURCHASE PRICE OF THE EQUIPMENT SOLD BY CANON USA AND CAUSING THE ALLEGED DAMAGE. WITHOUT LIMITING THE FOREGOING, YOU ASSUME ALL RISK AND LIABILITY FOR LOSS, DAMAGE OR INJURY TO YOU AND YOUR PROPERTY AND TO OTHERS AND THEIR PROPERTY ARISING OUT OF USE, MISUSE OR INABILITY TO USE THE EQUIPMENT NOT CAUSED DIRECTLY BY THE NEGLIGENCE OF CANON USA. (SOME STATES DO NOT ALLOW THE EXCLUSION OR LIMITATION OF INCIDENTAL OR CONSEQUENTIAL DAMAGES, SO THE ABOVE LIMITATION MAY NOT APPLY TO YOU).THIS WARRANTY SHALL NOT EXTEND TO ANYONE OTHER THAN THE ORIGINAL PURCHASER OF THIS EQUIPMENT OR THE PERSON FOR WHOM IT WAS PURCHASED AS A GIFT.

This warranty gives you specific legal rights, and you may also have other rights which vary from state to state.

CANON U.S.A., INC.

CANADA

CANON CONSUMER DIGITAL VIDEO EQUIPMENT LIMITED WARRANTY

The limited warranty set forth below is given by Canon Canada Inc. ("Canon Canada") with respect to Canon Consumer Digital Video Equipment (the "Equipment") purchased in Canada. This limited warranty is only effective upon presentation of a bill of sale or other proof of purchase for this Equipment to a Canon Service Facility when repairs are required.

The Equipment is warranted under normal, non-commercial, personal use, against defective materials or workmanship as follows:

Parts: Defective parts will be exchanged for new parts or, at Canon Canada's option, comparable rebuilt parts for a period of one year from the date of original purchase, except Video Heads which will be exchanged for a period of 3 months from the date of purchase.

Labour: For a period of one year from the date of original purchase, labour will be provided free of charge by our Canon Service Facilities in Canada.

This limited warranty covers all defects except where:

(a) The loss or damage to the product results from:

    i) accident, natural disaster, mishandling, abuse, neglect, unauthorized product modification or failure to follow instructions contained in the instruction manual;

    ii) the use of accessories, attachments, products, supplies, parts or devices with the Equipment that do not conform to Canon specifications or that cause abnormally frequent service problems;

    iii) repairs or services performed by any party other than a Canon Service Facility;

    iv) defective batteries or any exposure to water, sand or dirt;

    v) shipping (claim must be presented to the shipper);

(b) Any serial number on the video equipment is altered or removed.

(c) The Equipment is used for commercial, professional or industrial purposes.

This limited warranty does not cover the cabinet (exterior finish) of the Equipment, media, nor does it apply to Equipment purchased outside Canada.

If the Equipment contains a hard disk drive, Canon Canada recommends that data stored on that drive be duplicated or backed up to prevent its loss in the event of a failure or other malfunction of such drive.

TO OBTAIN WARRANTY SERVICE

Ship your Equipment in its original carton, box or equivalent, properly packed, fully insured with shipping charges prepaid, together with a copy of your bill of sale or other proof of purchase and a description of the problem to any of the Canon Service Facilities in Canada.

LIMITATIONS

Except as otherwise required by applicable legislation, this warranty is in lieu of all other warranties, conditions, guarantees or representations, express or implied, statutory or otherwise, relative to the Equipment, including implied warranties or conditions of merchantability or fitness for a particular purpose. Canon Canada assumes no liability for special, consequential or incidental damages, loss or corruption of data including, without limitation, data stored on the hard disk drive of the Equipment or loss that may arise, whether on account of negligence or otherwise, from the use, misuse or inability to use the Equipment (including loss of profit, revenue, media or enjoyment) or from failure to conform to any express or implied warranties, conditions, guarantees or representations. Any recovery under this limited warranty shall not exceed the purchase price of the equipment. Canon Canada does not assume or authorize any other person to assume for Canon Canada any other liability with respect to this equipment.

This warranty does not extend to any person other than the original purchaser of the Equipment or the person for whom it was purchased as a gift and states your exclusive remedy.

NOTICE TO CONSUMER

If you plan to take important videos or if the product has not been used for some time, please check all functions with the instruction book before using it.

Canon

Canon Inc.   30-2, Shimomaruko 3-chome, Ohta-ku, Tokyo 146-8501, Japan

---

USA

CANON U.S.A., INC. NEW JERSEY OFFICE
100 Jamesburg Road, Jamesburg, NJ 08831 USA

CANON U.S.A., INC. CHICAGO OFFICE
100 Park Blvd., Itasca, IL 60143 USA

CANON U.S.A., INC. LOS ANGELES OFFICE
15955 Alton Parkway, Irvine, CA 92618 USA

CANON U.S.A., INC. HONOLULU OFFICE
210 Ward Avenue, Suite 200, Honolulu, HI 96814 USA

❖ If you have any questions, call the Canon U.S.A.
   Information Center toll-free at 1-800-828-4040 (USA only).

• The information in this document in verified as of July 2017. Subject to change without notice.
  Visit your local Canon Web site to download the latest version.

PUB. DIE-0517-000

www.ingramcontent.com/pod-product-compliance
Lightning Source LLC
Chambersburg PA
CBHW081726220526
45468CB00008B/1987